Puppy Prepared?
The Roadmap to Getting Your Dream Dog

Sarah Bartlett KCAI CD R QIDTI

DEDICATION

For my Dad, Karen, Sam, Simon & Spencer, about to embark on
their journey with a new German Shepherd.
For my dogs past, present, future and for yours.

Puppy Prepared?

CONTENTS

ACKNOWLEDGMENTS

Massive thanks to Debbie, Lillie, Claire & Lou for helping me get this book over the final hurdles to make it actually legible! Big thanks to Lisa for allowing us to picture her puppies and also to Tim Bartlett - photographer and cover designer extraordinaire! As always thanks to my ever-suffering hubby, while I type into the dark of night.
My 8 puppies who have taught me so much, over the rainbow bridge - Rosco, Bella, Jazz & Merlin.
And to those still with us - Ziggy, Moss, Fern & Ripple.

1 PREFACE

What this book will/won't help you with

1st puppy, or 10th if it's a puppy in addition to existing dog or dogs you have at home currently, I strongly advise that you buy another of my books - 'Another Pup?' - The comprehensive guide to adding to or becoming a multi-dog household. Available direct from me or on amazon.

Having a puppy is bloomin' hard work! And it's not all cute fluff and cuddles.

This book will give you all the knowledge, tips and tricks you need to know to find your new super sidekick, your new best friend.

I'm going to take you through all the things to consider before you get your new family member. Choosing the right breed (or mix of) and the right breed type, down to which puppy in the litter is a good fit for you. How to puppy proof your home, what you need to buy, what to budget for both in terms of money and time. The differences between a good breeder and bad - and what affect this will have if you get it wrong. Picking a healthy puppy and much much more!

You have invested time and money into this book so you can get it right - massive pat on the back to you! Seriously, I'm not being condescending here! That's a massive step to ensure you get it right - more happy dogs and happy owners can only be a good thing.

There will be times that you start to wonder why you got a puppy... Yes really! This is going to happen and when it does you should know this is normal and natural and even I go through it with each new puppy I add to my family. Their hormones kick in after those initial sleepy totally cute first few weeks, we become tired of their abundant energy and our patience wains. We start to think we have got it wrong and wonder if we did the right thing.

I promise you, you will have these moments!

What we want to avoid, is this becoming more than just fleeting moments and becoming recurring thoughts over months and then you having to make the hard decision to give the dog up or live the next ten to fifteen years in misery with the wrong dog for you.

The sad truth is, this happens all the time. We all have the best intentions but often our initial excitement of getting a puppy and our lack of thought and research leads to misery.

This is book 1 of the Super Sidekick Series.

Book 2 will be taking you through your first year with pupster, what you need to teach them, how to live with them and how to get through those dreaded teenage hormones. Head over to Facebook and search @SarahBartlettDogTrainer to find out more and claim your free bonuses just for purchasing this book!

Why should you listen to me?

I have done it all wrong. I have paid the price, and unfortunately so have some of my dogs as I went along. I speak from experience, heart-breaking experience at times and I want to help you avoid all the things I had to go through so you can get it right first time.

Who the hell am I to tell you what you should and shouldn't do?

I have had 8 puppies of my own (not including ones I have bred) over the last 15 years, plus an additional 6 adult dogs not from pups. I am currently owned by 5 dogs and a pony, we were at 6 dogs, a pony and a cat until recently. We sadly lost our Goon, the Flatcoat Retriever that was Merlin and our old cat Dobi earlier this year (2019). I spend my days training dogs and their owners, most of these are puppies which is what has led me to write this book and the rest of the series.

I won't bore you with the long list of courses, workshops and seminars I have attended over the years, nor go through the thousands of dogs and owners I have helped over the last 12 years of running my business but those things along with my own experiences and failures has given me a right to show and guide you in the right direction to find the puppy for you and get you started on the right path - for the night is dark and full of terrors... or should I say the night is loud and full of puppy puddles and whines initially!

I want to share with you a couple of back stories before we progress, share with you a few things that, as you will see have been crucial to my learning and how and why things went wrong.

Let me take you back in time..

I got my first house a few weeks before my 18th birthday. First on the to do list was to acquire two dogs, a big one and a small one. My partner Chris and I at the time had already set our heart on what large dog we were getting, his parents had recently mated their Rottweiler bitch Macy, and we were waiting for 'our baby to arrive'.

I grew up with rescue mongrels' crossbreeds and the big dog would be a cross breed, I was working as a mechanical engineer at the time and other than my real love for dogs I knew next to nothing! We discussed smaller breeds I said I wanted either a chihuahua or a 'sausage dog' it didn't necessarily need to be a puppy, we were open to rescue and I had found what appeared to be a Bassett hound mix with a dachshund at Manchester dogs home, but he was snapped up before we could go and get him.

I was keen on a Chihuahua or a sausage dog because I have fond memories of friends' dogs of these breeds as a child.

I started looking in the local for sale ads newspaper 'The Loot' and looked for Dachshunds, it was only at this point that my boyfriend realised I wasn't talking about a Bassett hound and I in fact wanted a miniature Dachshund.

I'm not sure what tipped the balance from Chihuahua to Dachshund/sausage dog but that's the direction we went in.

Chris wasn't averse to a Dachshund but would have preferred a Bassett. The only adverts I could find in the Loot for Dachshunds were for miniature longhaired, when in fact we wanted a smooth haired. Chris was actually allergic to dogs, long haired dogs bringing out his allergies the most, but as we were so impatient he said "it's ok we will get a longhair and I'll pay for it to be shaved every month" (I cringe as I write this but it's the truth). Our logic at the time was we wanted both small and large dog to grow up together and we thought it may be best to have small dog first for a few weeks before 'big puppy' arrived to ensure that the big pup didn't eat the small one! Bwahahaha!! What can I say, I was young and naive?

We drove to Mold in Wales one morning and viewed this lovely little shaded red miniature longhaired puppy he was shown to us in a conservatory type area, though we could hear other dogs barking we were never shown where the puppy was kept, the others in the litter or the mother. But it was ok, he was Kennel Club registered - or so I thought at the time.

I handed over £500 and we took our little bundle of fur home. I cannot really remember what the first night was like, but I do remember that within 6 weeks of bringing him home Bella came home (big pup).

Bella was just 5 weeks old and not very well, Macy had rejected the pups by this age and Bella was not fully weaned so lots of chicken and rice, and TLC seemed to clear up the runny andsometimes bloody mess she was creating. I also remember saying to Chris that this had to be his dog because I already was fed up of clearing up the mess and not having a clue about housetraining, we had a very small two up two down end terrace but thankfully we had a fairly large fenced concrete yard area surrounding the house. When we left for work the pups were left in the house, loose together and I would regularly come home to chaos, not only mess from them going to the toilet but they managed to find my lipstick and smear it on themselves and over the cream carpets upstairs. But it was ok, they were cute as buttons and needed to keep themselves occupied, plus I didn't have the finances nor even thought about having someone to come in and check on them during the day.

When Rosco reached 16 weeks he became very ill, with sickness and diarrhoea. Numerous trips to the vets, administering medication and myself suffering with the flu too. Heartbreak happened when, unfortunately he died while on a drip at the vets, I was devastated, absolutely gutted.

I know I couldn't have done anymore for him then, despite not knowing much or as much as I do now, I didn't hesitate to get him to the vets. Bella was also a little loose in her poo and I asked for medication from the vets which cleared this up. Bella then of course had become 'my dog' and I started to take her to local dog training classes and I spent most waking and non-working hours playing and training her and walking her.

When Bella reached about 6 months of age, she became very itchy, biting herself to the point where she was making holes in herself. Numerous trips to the vets and tests over many months confirmed that she had allergies to grass, pollen, fungal spores and flea bites. She loved to run and chase a ball on grass, she was a very outdoors and active type of dog so this was a hard thing to deal with while still meeting her exercise needs.

We would regularly attend fun dog shows which she loved, we attended one at our local park and as we were going to leave the ring once a class had finished a large black scruffy looking dog pulled the lead out of its owners hand and lunged and barked and growled in Bella's face, no damage done and other than being annoyed at the owner I didn't think much more of it (she was 8 months of age at this point - her age is very relevant here as you will find in book 2). This happened at the beginning of the summer and we spent the rest of the summer attending other fun dog shows.

The same summer we went to a really big show in London (I think it was called the wet nose show) when I was visiting my Mum and Bella growled and lunged at a cocker spaniel next to her in the ring, this was very unusual for her, it had never happened before. I soon regained her focus, no harm done and thought nothing of it.

The next month we started attending some fun agility classes at the same location as her previous puppy classes. On arrival to the class Bella was growling at every dog who came near her, it was only at this point it started to cause a problem. The trainer gave me some tips on how to improve her behaviour, and after a discussion we realised the incident on the local park had affected her and the only reason she had been ok most of the times in between is because she was on antihistamines for her allergies which made her slightly drowsy, as the weather was turning we were trying to wean her off them as there were less pollens etc around.

Also, it became clear that she associated any busy area with lots of dogs (like you would see at a dog show) and felt threatened, so her behaviour was out of fear ….'I'm going to get you before you get me'. It was very unfortunate that the incident happened in what was her secondary fear period (more on this in book 2), so it had more of an effect than what it would at another age or time in her life.

As the weeks progressed, she became more settled but there were two dogs of the same age as her who, when off lead and working on the agility equipment would often make a beeline for her and come in her space and invite her to play. Bella would respond by barking and growling. After about 10 weeks of this training there was one evening when, from the second we walked in the building she was pulling me toward the other dogs, but this time her energy was totally different, I was nervous of letting her get too close in case she did something she shouldn't. The trainer could also see a change in her and instructed me and the two owners of the other two dogs who normally invite her to play to let the three off lead in the secure training area. Reluctantly we did and to my amazement the three of them charged around playing without a care in the world! The following week it was the training centre's Christmas party, fun dog games etc. I had only planned to take Ziggy, (oh yes…Ziggy had arrived when Bella was 6 months of age, from the same breeder as Rosco and he was a happy little chappy) because Bella would have found it too stressful, but after such a breakthrough I took the two of them and Bella won most of the classes. She had a great time. I know the trainers took pity on us and were pleased with the change in her, but I wasn't complaining.

Things to remember from this story, that I will revisit are –

- Because I knew one/some of that breed as a child means I need one in my life, or does it?
- Two dogs/puppies at the same time - the drawbacks and pit falls
- Crate training - should you?
- Settling for something due to impatience - is this wise?
- Puppy proofing your home
- Allergies / health issues - how to avoid these as much as possible and what they mean.
- Breeder choice
- Breed choice
- Age of puppy coming home
- Plan for when leaving your dog at home

Ziggy

We collected him from Lymm truck stop…but it was ok because we had previously met the breeders (doh!). Ziggy was 7 weeks old and also ended up getting into trouble with Bella when we were out at work. As they grew up a bit we purchased a bog-standard dog kennel (like the one the Peanuts cartoon dog Snoopy liked to lie on) and I would leave them outside in the yard with bones to chew on each day when we were out at work.

They had shelter, something to do and water, what more could they need eh? They were walked religiously, and I gave up my hobbies and social things that I took part in after work once the dogs arrived and spent most of my time with them.

I became a little obsessed you may call it. I was completing my advanced modern apprenticeship in electronics and electrical engineering at the time, so was at college one day a week. The only girl in the course, so other than chatting dogs with the tutor the only thing I could find to do at lunchtimes was hide out in the local library reading dog books, breed books, all about all the different types of dogs and of course training books, I would regularly take out 5 or 6 books each week all about dogs. I couldn't quench my thirst for the knowledge.

When Ziggy arrived, I was working Saturdays, running a local pet shop (mainly so I could get discount on dog food, treats, toys etc) it was very expensive having two dogs and a growing menagerie of guinea pigs, rabbits, birds etc. So from the moment Ziggy came home, he came and spent Saturdays with me at the pet shop. It was a tiny shop and was running at a loss, I had a few regulars who came in, mainly OAP's who would come in for some cat litter or bird feed. I would spend my time cleaning out the resident animals for sale and playing with, training and grooming my little lad.

We bonded so much, it was lovely, he is still with me now at 14 years, he's suffering a long list of health concerns but he's still spritely and has a real zest for life.

What did I do wrong with Ziggy? Bella was 6 months of age when Zig arrived and full of energy, I used to run her on the local park with her ball, constantly playing fetch, she loved nothing more than her ball and Ziggy right from 11/12 weeks of age would chase behind her back and forth for an hour each day. I remember taking him to the vets for something routine and saying to the vet that I'm sure I'm over exercising him. To which the vet replied don't be silly, he's a small dog, he will let you know when he's had enough…. I knew nothing about not overexerting them at a young age, just something my gut was telling me at the time but took the vets word as gospel and carried on. Sadly, at around 18 months of age he was diagnosed with arthritic hips. He has never been the type of dog to just stop when he's had enough, yes, some dogs do this but to this day Ziggy would go out and run around all day if I let him, and then he would suffer after.

Once Zig was about 6 months of age, I rescued an elderly and senile Doberman – Rolo. He was only with us for 5 months before his liver and kidneys gave out and we had to make the final decision for him. After we lost Rolo I decided three dogs was a nice number and went on the search for a shaded cream miniature longhaired Dach female, mainly because I liked the colour, the colour was pretty rare at the time. I had kept Ziggy entire and wanted some Ziggy pups as he was such a little character. By this time, we had some limited access to the internet and I contacted a few breeders online, spoke at length on email with one breeder who for whatever reason didn't end up having the pup we wanted or was going to have but suggested a friend of his who did.

We arranged with this breeder to meet her in a lay-by near Crewe. We drove in my little 2CV down to Crewe and I went and sat in the passenger seat of the breeder's car who passed me this puppy, she was 9 weeks old, the last one and cream but with this black dipstick tail…I was a little put off by the tail but Chris was in love so again we got our paperwork, puppy and handed over £550.

Jazz is what we called her, she was a very happy little character and it was around this time I finally opted to use a crate, for when I was out. Leaving the dogs outside wasn't working as the kids on the street would tease them through the bars of our fence in the day when we were not there.

I had one small crate for the two Dachs and eventually one larger one for the three of them. This isn't something I would advise now.. Nor most if not all of what I did during my early years of dog ownership!

When Ziggy was around 12 months of age, I started working at the place that I was taking Bella training, also the same place as the vets I used. I was working in the kennels there which meant I could not only walk the dogs to work I could leave them in the kennels while

I was working and exercise them in my breaks. Because Jazz was such a tender age, she couldn't go into the kennels yet and there was a day-care facility which at the time was being run by the trainer who had helped me with Bella, so Jazz spent her days in day-care, in expert hands.

Me working at the kennels didn't last long and I was left without a job and without an income to pay for my now large menagerie (26 rabbits 16 guinea pigs, an aviary full of birds, a hand reared living loose in the house cockatiel and a Pueblan milk snake) never mind three dogs, a house and car! I took the first job I could get, which unfortunately meant long hours in a call centre meaning 9-10 hours away from home each day. It also meant at 5am I was out walking my dogs for over an hour to ensure they were as tired as possible before I left for work. I'm ashamed to say that the three dogs were left for that time together, (please do not do this!) until I returned and walked them immediately. I just didn't have the finances to pay for help at the time but was not willing to give up on my dogs either. Over the following year I was getting more stressed hating my job, the hours I was working. Chris and I split up, then I had a string of pretty useless boyfriends, plus short term housemates who were meant to help out with the dogs while I was at work, needless to say – Bella's behaviour deteriorated and she became aggressive to other dogs and to some people. I was in denial about her aggression toward people as it was never in my presence, always when she was with other people. I called the same trainer for help, she had also left the establishment, but I had heard she was working for herself. She came out and was so pleased to hear from me, she wanted me to set up a dog walking company, many of her training clients wanted a dog walker and I could keep up the training that she had done with dogs and their owners. This was the start of Hound Helpers Ltd, the award-winning training and pet care business that I still run to this day.

Things to remember from this story, that I will revisit are –

- Making plan to spend the time to bond with your puppy
- Collecting a puppy from a lay-by or service station
- Planning for pet care when you can't be there, choosing who to trust

- Over exercise / walking your pup too much
- Preventing health problems
- The decision to breed from your dog or not
- How life changes, providing for our dogs in times of change
- Rare colours

There are many more stories I will share with you as we progress but I need to start helping you to understand why these were mistakes and what affect they have had to avoid me going into full 'once upon a time in Sarah land' mode!

Puppy Prepared?

2 **INTRODUCTION**

Still wondering why or how there is a whole book dedicated to finding the right puppy for you?

It's easy right? Money at the ready, find a breeder, buy it, take home, housetraining, cute puppy eyes and it grows into the dog you want yeah?

NO! A thousand nopes and some more nopes needed.

In the words of the good old girls of spice…. Stop right there, thank you very much!

There are a few facts I need to tell you –

- Puppies are not clean slates
- Every single dog is different, even within the same breed and even in the same litter
- Having a mongrel, crossbreed, Heinz 57 or 'bitsa' is no guarantee of health, temperament or longevity
- Dogs are not the same as how you remember them as a child
- Some breeds are not suited to ever be a pet dog without a job to do.
- Having a puppy from rescue isn't necessarily the answer
- Because you like your friends' dog of the same breed or mix of breeds does not mean you should have one or that you

will find one the same.
- Breeders can always be doing more to make your life and pups life easier, even the best of breeders have room for improvement - myself included!
- Convenience does not necessarily equal happiness
- Higher price does not mean a better-quality pup in many cases

I could go on and on, and to a certain extent I will throughout the book, but I will explain the what, why and how.

In my honest opinion it's too easy to buy a puppy and it's too easy to breed puppies which in turn unfortunately means you are automatically on the back foot and set up to get a pup that isn't right for you. In my opinion lack of education for both dog owners and for breeders is the real reason for so many dogs in rescue.

Most dogs in rescue are between the ages of 6 months and 2 years - because they have been the wrong dog for that home/family/environment. If some more time and care and energy had been put into researching the right dog and type of breed for them and what that would involve there wouldn't be half as many dogs given up.

I'm here to help turn that around in whatever small way I can. Once you have read and digested everything, please pass this book around your soon to be dog owning friends, the more hands it reaches the better it will be for all involved.

The unfortunate truth and the whole reason for writing this book is: Most people put more effort, time and research into buying a car which they will likely only have for 5 years. Yes, I accept that a car is normally a higher priced item than a puppy but if we think about it, let's compare the differences.

Car buying and selection process;

- Research badge/brand reliability & reputation
- Decide on what model or car type is practical for your lifestyle, what you expect to do with it - ie a hatchback, 4x4,

saloon or an estate etc
- You may have looked at the price and availability of parts if it breaks
- You will be looking at what possible life changes you expect to have over the next few years and if the car will suit your changing needs
- What fuel, engine type and gearbox you want/need will be considered
- Look into how economical it is for the types of driving you will be doing with it
- You will have a preference on colour or at least an idea what colours you definitely wouldn't have
- You will look into how much they are and where you can find the best deals for the age you are looking at.
- Most will look at insurance costs
- Most will look into what optional extras you can get - some of which may be deal breakers, if you can't have aircon or Bluetooth connectivity for example.
- Once you have considered all of the above, you will go for a test drive. You will sit in it.
- Is it comfy, does it meet your needs in person as much as it does on paper? You will drive it, reverse it and get a real feel for the vehicle.

For many car buyers there will be even more factors considered, and yes, I hold my hands up I'm just as fussy if not more fussy when it comes to vehicles as the next person (despite my love for Citroen 2CV's - yes I am a car geek, and proud!)

But let me say again… all of this research and time invested in getting something which is not a living thing, nor does it live in the house with you and is very unlikely to spend more than 5 years in your possession. We sell cars after a while, for a lesser price than what we paid but we do all of this still knowing we will get some of our money back!

A puppy could be with you for 15 years, in your home as your faithful companion. Getting it right is the difference between making or breaking quality of life for either you or your dog over that time.

Most puppy owners go from wanting a puppy to one arriving in less than a month, and over half of those it's under a fortnight. I have done this too. It's really tempting! Money in the bank, immediate access to the internet and a long list of breeders with puppies available to bring home now.

Over 80% of dogs I see professionally for training are the wrong dog or choice for that home and while most of them we can and do make it work. Life would have been easier had the research and thought been put in, in the first place.

Less than 25% of puppy buyers visit more than one breeder or visit the pups more than once, meaning they see the puppy for the first time and within a couple of hours are taking them home with them.

I get how hard it is to visit a litter of puppies when they are ready to come home, and you have money burning in your pocket and not bring one home. Those adorable cute eyes pleading with you. It's one of the hardest things you can ever do, but please do not do this! At the very least come home without pup and sleep on it, refer to the tick list you will make after reading this book and if things don't feel right or add up you know not to return.

What is another 100miles, another £100 or a few more weeks or months to wait if its means getting it right and a happy life for what could be 15 years or more with your new puppy?

A dog is not a dog is a dog… What?

I grew up with crossbreeds or mongrels for want of a better word, dogs that we could pretty accurately guess at possibly 50% of their genetic makeup but the rest was a mystery, they were rescues. Pedigree breeds were not something that were common place in my area other than the odd Labrador or Jack Russell type (which interestingly, the Jack Russell Terrier has only become a recognised and registered pedigree over the last few years). I was of the opinion that I now see is most people's view, that a dog is a dog, you make it what you want, and they just differ in size, shape, colour and coat type, breed doesn't affect anything much other than looks - this really isn't true! And I can't stress this fact enough.

Yes, we can mould and shape our dogs to a certain extent but there is so much that we cannot control. Most of which you will find the more you read but please, please, please even if you give up reading now - just remember this one fact if nothing else.

All breeds and breed types have been bred in the past for a specific purpose or job, and they still have a want and need to perform these activities now, many years and generations later it's their instinct. Dogs who are not provided with a way to perform their natural instincts become problem dogs and go what I call 'self-employed' and get themselves and often their owners and guardians into trouble.

Changes in society, and how dogs haven't adjusted yet

Many puppy buyers also have very fond memories of the dog they had as a child, or a family dog, and look to get something the same or similar, even if it's not the same breed they hope for something of a similar temperament and character as it was more than likely that that was the start of their love of dogs and that dog is their idea of an ideal family companion. I love to look back and think about Sheba, Penny, Sadie and the other dogs I had as a child and in the family but each of them would not fit into life in this day and age.

Even over the last 20 years things have changed rapidly for human life and with it so has what we expect of dogs. Gone are the days where we were told to not go near the dog if they were eating or sleeping - now it seems that a dog is not permitted to even grumble at a child, even if they are being bounced on. It is a very sad state of affairs and something I could wax lyrical on, but I won't.

The family dog that had company from the Mum of the family all day, who was included in most activities and got to go out and roam as much as its heart was content is now not practical nor legal in the UK (the roaming part at least). Society has more of a want it now/yesterday mentality and we all work long hours leaving our beloved companions at home without stimulation for longer periods. Life is faster in general and allowing the time for a puppy to acclimatise to this isn't always practical nor feasible.

We are always rushing or distracted on our phones - leaving little time for interacting and bonding with our dogs - all of which has an effect on our lives with them.

You are still not going to get perfection in a pup

Now I have to say that if you are expecting your puppy to be perfect you are in fact deluded and are in for a fall. However, the perfect puppy for you is, of course within reach. Only if you are armed with the right knowledge and research.

Consider this.

Are you the perfect example of a human being? In form function and character?

What makes something perfect? Who decides what is perfect or in fact normal?

Ok, so to avoid me going down this particular rabbit hole I will stop here but hopefully it has got you thinking about what perfect means to you and also limiting your expectations of your puppy.

I had very high expectations and wishes!

I grew up watching Lassie, Flipper, Free Willy, Andre, Skippy, Balto and all the kind of 'Disney-esque' programs and films that had panted the picture of the animal best friend, who would lay down their life for you, who would always want to be with you and be glued to your side. While I acknowledge me being raised as an only child will have formed some of my over attachment to the idea of an animal companion that I think, I felt subconsciously fill the sibling void I did have every expectation of the relationship between me and my dog being very similar to all of this. Whether or not this is a surprise to you I have yet to really get that kind of bond. Dogs like their own space too, they don't understand – "Get Bud Lassie" and the English language as these programs led me to believe. Dogs will also look after themselves first as loyal as they are, they will look after number one if pushed far enough.

The more research I did for this book the more I realised that I am not the only one who embarked on their first puppy search with the mental image of the bond between Bud, Sandy and Lassie or between Flipper and Porter and its more common than you would think.

The films portrayed something that isn't achievable or at least not in that way but it's worth remembering that you can in fact create a very special bond between you and your puppy/dog, but it takes work, it takes time, it takes patience. You are required to throw all of these notions and preconceptions out of the window to look at and get to know the dog in front of you. Not the dog you wish you had instead.

If you haven't noticed already, I am full of quirks, and guess what? My dogs are too.

I will say it again, my dogs are not perfect, and neither am I – but they are perfect for me.

Puppy Prepared?

3 BREED TYPES, TRAITS AND INSTINCTS - THEY MATTER!

There are hundreds of pedigree breeds across the world, we have over 200 breeds recognised by the kennel club in the UK, and many more breeds that aren't recognised both within the uk and abroad

There are 7 groups of breeds of pedigree dogs and the 200 plus breeds registered by the kennel club in the UK are spread across these groups.

Each group has an overview of a job or role that the dogs within it were originally bred for and then each breed within that was bred for a more specific task or purpose.

Did you know the Dobermann was originally the taxman's dog? To protect and intimidate? That a Dalmatian was originally bred to run between the wheels of a horse and carriage for many miles a day? That the Rhodesian Ridgeback was bred to hunt lions, the Dachshund to hunt badgers and the Labrador was originally the Fisherman's dog before it was a Retriever on the shooting field?

There are also a few subgroups within each group which I will list a few as examples

I cannot list each dog within each category so I will stick to a handful of the most popular and well known within each.

Gundog
*Also known as the sporting group in America and overseas

Naturally active and alert, gun dogs make likeable, well-rounded companions. First developed to work closely with hunters to locate and/or retrieve quarry. There are four basic types of Sporting dogs; spaniels, pointers, retrievers and setters. Known for their superior instincts in water and woods, many of these breeds enjoy hunting and other field activities. Many of them, especially the water-retrieving breeds, have well insulated water repellent coats, which are quite resilient to the elements. This is one of the most popular groups in the UK and for good reason, particularly the spaniel and retriever breeds are very well suited to the terrain we have in the UK, more so for countryside dwelling owners and are amongst some of the most sociable adaptable breeds out there.

Subgroups

Retrievers
Labrador Retriever
Golden Retriever
Flatcoat Retriever
Chesapeake Bay Retriever
Curlycoat Retriever
Nova Scotia Duck Tolling Retriever

Yes, there are six different types of Retriever, but what most people think of when we hear 'I have a Retriever' is that they mean they have a Golden Retriever.

Spaniels -
Cocker
Springer

There are countless different types of spaniel from the Brittany to the Sussex to the Irish water spaniel, all in different coat types, colours and sizes and all with slightly different histories and purposes on the shooting field

HPR (Hunt Point and Retrieve)
Weimaraner
German Shorthaired Pointer
Hungarian Vizsla

There are many others who won't fit into these sub categories, some who will just hunt and point such as English Pointers or for example Setters are not bred to retrieve but to hunt and point there are Red and White Setters, English Setters, Gordon Setters, not just the Irish/Red Setter that you may think of when hearing the word setter.

Terrier

Feisty and energetic are two of the primary traits that come to mind for those who have experience with Terriers. In fact, many describe their distinct personalities as "eager for a spirited argument." Bred to hunt, kill vermin and to guard their family's home or barn; sizes range from fairly small, as in the Norfolk, Cairn or West Highland White Terrier, to the larger and Airedale Terrier. Interestingly Airedales were originally bred as fighting dogs down the mines. Prospective owners should know that terriers can make great pets, but they do require determination on the part of the owner because they can be stubborn; have high energy levels, and many require special grooming (known as "stripping") to maintain a characteristic appearance.

Popular breeds in this group;

Westie / West Highland White Terrier
Cairn (like Toto on the wizard of oz)
Staffy / Staffordshire Bull Terrier
Jack Russell

Hound

Most hounds share the common ancestral trait of being used for hunting. Some use acute scenting powers to follow a trail. Others demonstrate a phenomenal gift of stamina as they relentlessly run down quarry. Beyond this, however, generalisations about hounds are hard to come by, since the Group encompasses quite a diverse lot. There are Pharaoh Hounds, Norwegian Elkhounds, Afghans and Beagles, among others. Some hounds share the distinct ability to produce a unique sound known as baying. You'd best sample this sound before you decide to get a hound of your own to be sure it's your cup of tea - it is not mine I can tell you that much! Thank fully Dachs do not bay.

Subgroups -

Sight hounds (bred to hunt on sight of movement)
Greyhound
Whippet
Saluki

Scent hounds (bred to follow and hunt from a scent)
Beagle
Dachshund
Bassett Hound
Blood Hound

Pastoral
*Also known as the herding group

All Herding breeds share an instinctual ability to control the movement of other animals. These breeds were developed to gather, herd and protect livestock. Today, some like the Belgian Malinois and the German Shepherd Dog are commonly used for police and protection work and many would think they belong in the working group rather than in a herding category but their original purpose was to be livestock herders as well as guardians so it these breeds are still categorised as such. The herding instinct in these breeds is so strong that many of these breeds have been known to gently herd their owners, especially the children of the family. In general, these are highly intelligent dogs, which isn't always what we want - intelligence doesn't necessarily make them easy for us dog owners. Teaching the wrong thing once can often result in the dog never forgetting and so never learning to do what we actually want them to do. They can make excellent companions and respond beautifully to training exercises if trained carefully and given a job or an outlet for their strong heading instincts. These dogs are rarely suitable to the first-time dog owner.

Common breeds in this group -

German Shepherd / GSD
Collie/sheepdog
Old English Sheepdog (Dulux dog)
Corgi
Sheltie / Shetland Sheepdog

There are also four types of Belgian Shepherd/BSD - Malinois (short hair) most popular due to portrayal in films etc. Malinois are also known as 'Malligators'… and that is for very good reason. Definitely not a breed for a pet! GSDs & BSDs and a lot of herding breeds also guard, they definitely need careful consideration

Utility
*non sporting as it's known as overseas

Utility dogs are made up of a diverse group of breeds with varying sizes, coats, personalities and overall appearance. They come from a wide variety of backgrounds, so it is hard to generalize about this group of dogs. The differences in features can be vast. Most are good watchdogs and housedogs.

Popular breeds in this group;

French Bulldog
Dalmatian
Poodle

Lhasa Apso

Toy

Toy breeds might be short on size, but they are definitely not short on personality! Breeds in the Toy group are affectionate, sociable and adaptable to a wide range of lifestyles. Just don't let their size and winsome expressions fool you: they are smart full of energy and many have strong protective instincts. Toy dogs are popular with city dwellers because they make ideal apartment dogs and terrific lap warmers on nippy nights.

Common breeds -
Pug
Chihuahua
Bichon frise
Shihtzu

And a few more to throw you with their breed names... you may think they belong in other categories, but they do not, they are in fact part of the toy group –

Cavalier King Charles Spaniel
Italian greyhound
Yorkshire terrier

Working

Quick to learn, dogs of the Working Group are intelligent, strong, watchful, and alert. Bred to assist man, they excel at jobs such as guarding property, pulling sleds and performing water rescues. Doberman Pinschers, Siberian Huskies and Great Danes are part of this Group, to name just a few. They make wonderful companions but because they are large, and naturally protective, prospective owners need to know how to properly train and socialize a dog. Some breeds in the Working Group may not be for the first-time dog owner

Common breeds
Boxer
Rottweiler
Dobermann
Siberian Husky

Each breed has instincts that have been bred into them, bred selectively over many generations to enable them to fulfil their purpose or job. These instincts can either be a blessing or a curse so do not discount their desire to fulfil their need to perform these tasks and activities. Commonly I see owners of young Dobermanns complaining that at around 7-10 months of age they won't stop barking at people walking past the property. This is simply the dog doing what it was bred to do, to protect and intimidate any perceived threats to its property or people. Another example is a Sheepdog/Border Collie in a pet home where, as it matures it starts to herd the young children and nip at their ankles. In simple terms the dog is without a herd of sheep to round up and it has replaced sheep with children, it has a deep and strong desire to round up anything that moves and will do, unless it is given a suitable outlet for its instincts. I cannot stress enough how important it is to pick the right breed or mix of breeds for you - it can and does go wrong regularly. Hence the overwhelming number of young dogs in rescue.

A note on Gundogs

This group is the biggest group of dogs, the most variety of breeds and often the most suited to busy family life. These dogs more than in any other group have been bred to be sociable, to work alongside people and dogs all day long in the working shooting field, any signs of a 'hard mouth' or aggression are certainly not desirable in this group for any of the breeds, they are bred to be biddable. Now I'm not saying this is the easiest option, but you have more chance of getting a dog who will adjust to family life and be able to join in with long walks and hikes with the family than many other breeds from other groups.

I see more Labradors for training than any other breed and normally under the age of 3. We mustn't forget that yes, they are a highly popular breed so of course the law of averages dictates I will see a high percentage of them. But the point I'm making here is they are not the easiest dog to live with when they are young and bouncy without the right foundations, mental stimulation and exercise.

There are a handful of dog breeds that were literally just bred to be a companion, to sit on laps and comfort their owners. Amongst these are the Cavalier King Charles Spaniel, the French Bulldog and the Italian Greyhound. Most breeds (not that there are many) that were bred for this purpose are unfortunately now the victims of many health problems (more on this in a later chapter) but if you want something to chill out with, take a short stroll with and to be your hot water bottle and companion with little stress or hassle then this may be worth looking into - keeping health issues to the forefront of your mind.

Designer dogs / Popular crossbreeds / Doodles etc

Over the last decade there has been a huge influx of crossbreeds being bred. The most popular varieties being the Labradoodle and the Cockerpoo.

There is a common train of thought that these dogs will be healthier when in fact this does not appear to be the case. Most I see at best suffer with recurring ear infections (mainly due to their mix of coat type and the hair growing in their ear canals) and at worst suffer serious health issues such as hip dysplasia and blindness due to both breeds that they are a mixed of suffering the same health concerns, which has doubled the issue with the cross if not bred responsibly.

The draw to these dogs seems to also be about being apparently hypoallergenic and non-shedding… however…

The main things to remember about these designer dogs / crosses are as follows

- You are mixing instincts and it will never result in a 50/50 split of what you will get from each breed
- You are mixing coat types, particularly with poodle crosses there is no guarantee if the resulting puppies will indeed be the type that doesn't shed or if in fact they are hypoallergenic, there may only be one in each litter that is in fact non shedding and not going to aggravate your allergies
- Most breeders of these crosses are not in it for the betterment of the breed as it is not a breed and have got into breeding them for a quick buck. They do not have to keep to any rules or guidelines as they cannot register the puppies to any organisation worth the paper it's written on.
- Poodle crosses are often high maintenance with their coats and will be hard work to keep mat free and comfortable. Many trips to the grooming salon is required throughout its lifetime.
- Allergies are commonplace in these crossbreeds. I'm not sure whether its due to their mix of breeds or from irresponsible rearing on the breeder's part but for whatever the reason this is a very common and expensive issue.
- Health tests should still be done for both parents

In my opinion although many are lovely and great pet dogs, there are just as many or more who are not, the cute fluff ball of a puppy does not turn out to be what owners imagined.

Again, mainly on the Poodle crosses front, while I'm not against Poodles in the slightest they are a wonderful breed. Poodles are highly intelligent and mixing this with a working or Gundog type breed often makes for a very mischievous dog, that aren't the easiest to train as they will often outwit their owners and get into bad habits.

Their coats mat very easily which then is cause for friction often between groomers and owners when the groomers opt for the kinder option of clipping the fur short, rather than the alternative of putting the dog through hell and pulling at the coat which from the top looks fine but is actually matted at the skin and suffocating for the dog.
This is not aimed to put you off a cross breed, if anything I think through the popularity of these we may start to see the return of the

good old Heinz 57 in the not so distant future, which would be great but if you get one you need to do even more research than what you would for a pedigree and you need to be a fan of grooming your dog daily (or have it scalped/shaved short regularly).

Getting to know the breed, not just one individual

Breeds - just because your friend has one or because they look cute does not mean that you should get one of that breed. There are exceptions to every rule and breed, and your friends dog may be it!

Just like you will spend time test driving a car, getting a feel for it before purchasing, do the same with your choice of breed (or mix of breeds).

Spend some time getting to know your breed of choice or if you haven't decided yet spend time with all the breeds you are interested in. The best way to do this is to join some breed specific groups on social media such as Facebook, attend some group walks, dog shows, maybe even a breed seminar, you will find lots of breed people at these events to talk to and you will learn more about your breed and what to look for in the parents of your pup. You could attend Crufts or Discover Dogs, these are two big events where you can meet many breeds and speak to owners and breeders (links to these events in Chapter 20).

Yes, breed specific books will also help you and I will always encourage you to purchase and read these, they will give you an idea. If, once you have done this you are still keen on the breed then this is when I would suggest and advise you do go and find some of that breed and spend some actual time with the breed 'in person' and get to know them.

Breed tunnel vision, owners will be protective

For most if not all breeds you will find bias, both for and against the breed.

Against? Really?

Well not against the breed as such, but against anyone other than them or someone who has owned the breed before having one, they are protective, they understand that their breed can be hard work and have seen it go wrong in some homes before. They want to protect puppies of 'their breed' from being passed around due to lack of understanding of the specific needs and traits of their breed. But of course, we have all got to start somewhere, all of these people had to have a first!

This is fairly common on Facebook groups and when contacting breeders directly. By offering to get to know the breed, asking for help with this to help you decide if you are making the right decision you will start to get them on side and at the same time actually get to know the breed, the reality of them and help you decide if they really are the right breed for you. If you are spending time with one breeder, know that even some traits, style of the breed maybe specific to that one kennel/breeder so it is worth spending time with different breeders and dogs from different breed lines.

Grooming considerations

Short hair, long hair, wire haired, double coated, curly coated - the list of coat types goes on.

Something that most dog owners don't put too much thought into, even when they have fallen in love with a heavy or long coated breed, it's more for the love of the look of them that they want the dog. However, without learning about how to care for that coat they will not end up looking how you want them to in the long run.

All dogs need some form of grooming, even short haired breeds need some amount of coat care, just as the hairless types need skin care and some form of grooming, really!

Each breed organisation or council will give you more accurate information on how to groom the dog but please do not purchase a pup without considering the grooming needs first. Even breeds that need to visit the pamper parlour regularly will still require you to put some effort in in-between appointments. Again, it comes down to researching what is required for the breed, what equipment its best, how long and how often you should be grooming your dog for each time and how often they should be professionally groomed. We will come onto cost implications of this soon.

Working versus Show Type

Just to complicate matters!

For many more common and popular breeds there are two types in each breed, Cockers, Labs, Golden Retrievers to name a few. Differences in coat length, intelligence, health and looks. There are pros and cons for both types.

Many people don't realise there is more than one type of breed within a pedigree breed. Their looks can be like chalk and cheese as can their behaviour and needs. Golden retrievers (show type) are the most common type that you will see on the park and at training classes, they have been bred to be more white than golden in recent years, they are long coated and have very broad heads, thick boned and heavy in both weight and appearance. The working type Goldie is totally different, slighter build, a deep golden red colour, considerably less hair in length and thickness. As a very general rule the working type of any breed is more intelligent, lighter build, very active and again as a general rule with less health issues.

Why is this? Show type strains of breeds are often line bred or have been bred very closely to type breeding ever closer to be in line with what is called a breed standard. At a show dogs are judged in relation to these standards and the closest example to the standard wins each class.

An example breed standard is as follows -

The Golden Retriever (Taken from the KC website)

General Appearance
Symmetrical, balanced, active, powerful, level mover; sound with kindly expression.
Characteristics
Biddable, intelligent and possessing natural working ability.
Temperament
Kindly, friendly and confident.
Head and Skull
Balanced and well chiselled, skull broad without coarseness; well set on neck, muzzle powerful, wide and deep. Length of foreface approximately equals length from well-defined stop to occiput. Nose preferably black.
Eyes
Dark brown, set well apart, dark rims.
Ears
Moderate size set on approximate level with eyes.
Mouth
Jaws strong, with a perfect, regular and complete scissor bite, i.e. upper teeth closely overlapping lower teeth and set square to the jaws.
Neck
Good length, clean and muscular.
Forequarters
Forelegs straight with good bone, shoulders well laid back, long in blade with upper arm of equal length placing legs well under body. Elbows close fitting.
Body
Balanced, short-coupled, deep through heart. Ribs deep, well sprung. Level topline.
Hindquarters
Loin and legs strong and muscular, good second thighs, well bent stifles. Hocks well let down, straight when viewed from rear, neither turning in nor out. Cow-hocks highly undesirable.
Feet

Round and cat-like.

Tail

Set on and carried level with back, reaching to hocks, without curl at tip.

Gait/Movement

Powerful with good drive. Straight and true in front and rear. Stride long and free with no sign of hackney action in front.

Coat

Flat or wavy with good feathering, dense water-resisting undercoat.

Colour

Any shade of gold or cream, neither red nor mahogany. A few white hairs on chest only, permissible.

Size

Height at withers: dogs: 56-61 cms (22-24 ins); bitches: 51-56 cms (20-22 ins).

Faults

Any departure from the foregoing points should be considered a fault and the seriousness with which the fault should be regarded should be in exact proportion to its degree and its effect upon the health and welfare of the dog and on the dog's ability to perform its traditional work.

Note

Male animals should have two apparently normal testicles fully descended into the scrotum.

*Note for prospective puppy buyers

Size – the Kennel Club Breed Standard is a guide and description of the ideal for the breed; the size as described does not imply that a dog will match the measurements given (height or weight). A dog might be larger or smaller than the size measurements stated in the Breed Standard.

The tighter the breeding (when looking at a dogs heritage or pedigree you can see the same dogs behind both the sire/father and dam/mother) this means that they are inbred to a certain extent, of course all pedigree breeds are inbred, this is how we create breeds in the first place, breeding similar dogs to each other until each litter is similar to each other. The extent of this does matter though (more on this in chapter 8). Working types however have normally been bred to their working ability rather than their looks. A dog who is successful at performing its job is usually very healthy, if it wasn't it wouldn't be working. If it didn't have a good temperament it wouldn't be working either.

There are drawbacks to both strains of whichever breed you choose. A working type or strain if you aren't planning on giving them a job, sport or excessive amounts of exercise will find ways to become 'self-employed' becoming destructive or getting themselves into trouble, climbing the walls and getting very frustrated which makes them very hard to live with.

Show types – usually lower energy or exercise needs and less intelligent which can make them easier to live with but they can be prone to more health issues, if long coated more grooming and not always the best temperament as this may not have been a primary factor to the breeder when mating two dogs to produce puppies, confirmation or being close the breed standard is the primary concern – if you are purchasing from a breeder who shows of course. There are exceptions and some lovely very responsible show breeders out there though unfortunately this isn't usually the ones who have the champion dogs or Crufts winners.

Having an intelligent dog makes them easy to train right?

Not necessarily, no.

The train of thought of 'my dogs Dad is a champion, field trials or show champion'. Although it's something nice to brag to your friends about, this is totally irrelevant unless you want to compete in these sports with your dog. Having a puppy from two working or field trials spaniels as a pet dog is not advisable unless you plan to spend every waking moment keeping them busy.

Puppy Prepared?

4 COST IMPLICATIONS

How much does caring for a dog really cost?

Dogs can be surprisingly expensive as there are a lot of costs that some owners may not have considered.

You should expect your dog to cost you at least £6,500 - £17,000 over their whole lifetime:

- Small dog breeds: £6,500 to £12,000
- Medium dog breeds: £8,500 to £13,000
- Large dog breeds: £7,400 to £17,000

This estimated lifetime cost is the minimum that you will need to care for your dog. It will vary according to your dog's size, breed and how long they live. Your dog could cost you as much as £33,000 over their lifetime if you decide or need to spend more on their ongoing care!

This estimated cost doesn't include the cost of any vet fees if your dog becomes ill, although the figures do include the cost of pet insurance. If your dog has an accident or develops a health problem, the cost of caring for them could increase dramatically. It's important to be prepared for this.

These are estimated minimum costs as a starting point. A crucial part of planning for a puppy is to sit down and work out a budget for them, considering your lifestyle and all the things your new dog may need.

Getting started: the initial cost of getting a dog

When you first get a dog, you'll also need to get everything they need to be happy and healthy.

This includes things like:

- Bed (and or crate)
- Coat, lead, collar and tag
- Food and water bowls
- Toothbrush and toothpaste
- Toys
- Car restraint
- Initial course of vaccinations
- Monthly wormers until your dog is 6 months old
- Neutering
- Microchipping (if this has not been done by the breeder).

The estimated costs for these are:

- Small dog breeds: £370
- Medium dog breeds: £390
- Large dog breeds: £425

This cost doesn't include the cost of buying a dog.

Monthly care: the ongoing cost of looking after your dog

Each month you need to budget for lots of things that your dog will need, such as:

- Yearly health checks and booster vaccinations
- Regular flea and worm treatments

- Pet insurance
- Food
- Small toy allowance
- Poo bags
- Toothpaste.

The estimated monthly costs for the above items are:

- Small dog: £70
- Medium dog: £80
- Large dog: £105

Even though you might buy some of these things as part of the initial cost, there are lots of things that you will need to keep buying over your dog's lifetime.

What's not included in the above figures and costings -

These numbers are all estimated and don't include the cost of purchasing a dog or vet fees if your dog becomes ill.

It also doesn't include other services for your dog that might be required depending on your lifestyle and experience, such as the cost of boarding kennels, training classes and any day care needed for your dog. If you think you'll need these, remember to budget for them as well.

The statistics and costings in this chapter were kindly provided by the PDSA.

Groomers and/or grooming equipment

This is a hard one for me to provide you with figures for as much depends on your area, and also the size of your dog, what coat type they have and how well you manage the coat. The bigger the dog, the more matting and the more you ask of your professional groomer the more it will cost. Some breeds such as poodles should be visit the grooming salon every 4-6 weeks where wire hair breeds once or twice a year for hand stripping.

A Labrador bath and de-shed treatment can range from £25 to £50. I see some Labs for grooming every month, where others I may only see once a year. Although they are a short-coated breed they still moult and with the change of seasons this can really become an issue in the house.

A working type Cocker spaniel with minimal feathers/fluffy bits can range from £30-45 and usually require around 4 times a year. Whereas a working type Cocker should be groomed every 8 weeks and prices can vary from £35 - £60 each time.

Giant, heavy coated breeds such as a Newfoundland can range from £60 (if you are lucky!) to £150 per time and this should be every 8 weeks.

Once you have your shortlist of breeds, I would advise you to call around your local grooming salons and ask them for a quote for grooming for an adult of your breed, plus how often they advise appointments being made.

You will need to purchase grooming equipment for you to keep their skin and coat healthy. Again, the breed you decide upon will have an influence on this, but the most basic items are -

A comb
Slicker brush
Nail clippers
Ear/eye wipes
Dog towels
Shampoo (please do not use shampoo for humans).

You can usually get the absolute basics for around £30 in total so this will need to be factored into costings for your first year with puppy.

Neutering/Spaying

This largely depends on the size of the dog you finally decide upon. Smaller breeds are cheaper than larger breeds to have spayed or neutered and in general male dogs are slightly cheaper to have neutered than bitches are to get spayed as it's a less invasive procedure.

I would not advise having your dog spayed or neutered under the age of 12 months, despite the fact that many vets advise otherwise. The reasons for this are something I cover more in Book 2.

It can cost between £110 to £230 to castrate a male dog and between £154 to £397 to spay female dog, based on research done by Bought by Many Pet Insurance.

Vaccinations (WSAVA Guidelines)

I am fairly anti - vaccine myself, this however is a very personal choice.

The World Small Animal Veterinary Association (WSAVA) provide the vaccination guidelines to all vets across the globe. Unfortunately not enough vets are picking up on the changes from when this was last updated in 2016. The current guidelines state that puppy vaccinations should be administered, a booster at around a year of age and then no more frequent than every three years thereafter for vaccinations for the core diseases such as Distemper, Parvo Virus and Bordatella. Unfortunately, most practices are still pushing for these diseases to be vaccinated against on an annual basis, throughout their lifetimes.

Feel free to research this further by following this link and maybe even quoting it or printing it out to give to your vet if they advise otherwise -
https://www.wsava.org/WSAVA/media/Documents/Guidelines/WSAVA-Vaccination-Guidelines-2015.pdf

Yearly boosters can cost anywhere between £35 and £75 in the

UK, the puppy course also in this price bracket.

More on vaccinations, diseases and socialisation etc in chapter 13

Insurance

Your breeder will often provide you with 4-6 weeks free insurance, though I would encourage you to think about considering taking out insurance for after this period.

The average annual premium for pet insurance costs UK dog owners £287 - equating to just over £23.90 per month, according to Consumer Intelligence data from quotes between May 2017 and May 2018. Research company Mintel gives a slightly higher figure of £324 for annual premiums in 2017, based on data from the Association of British Insurers. These figures are from Bought by Many.

Not only does pet insurance offer you peace of mind when things go wrong and vet bills are mounting up, it also offers peace of mind if your dog causes an accident. Pet insurance also covers you for public liability. If your dog, for example got free and caused a road traffic accident you or the person in charge of the dog at the time would be held liable for all cost incurred. If you do not have public liability cover then this can result in you losing your home to pay the bill which can easily reach over £500k. If you decide against pet insurance, I would strongly suggest you do one of the following instead to ensure you have some form of public liability. Check your home insurance policy as this sometimes does give you such cover outside of the home as well as within - though please check the small print. The other option is to take out membership with The Dogs Trust for only £25 a year (or £12.50 if you're over 60). Amongst other benefits this offers 3rd party public liability insurance for your dog – up to £1,000,000 per claim if your dog causes damage or injury to another person, their property or pets (an excess of £200 applies for the UK and £500 in the Republic of Ireland).

Many insurance companies also offer a set amount per year for 'complementary therapies', it is worth getting cover for this where possible as these therapies can be crucial in a dog's recovery from serious illness or injury.

Pet insurance just like any other insurance will mean increased premiums once you have claimed, in the following policy year, and beyond.

Some breeds and cross breeds will be in higher insurance brackets if they are at high risk of breed specific health problems or if they are a breed who doesn't live a long life - giant breeds are a good example of this as many do not often make it to ten years of age. Once your dog reaches a certain age, insurance premiums will increase too as they are getting older and more susceptible to health problems (much like us). Dogs are classed as 'veteran' once over the age of 7. Once above this age you can expect the premiums to increase with each policy year. They will often ask you to pay a percentage of each claim on top of the excess once above a certain age too - something to keep in mind and watch for.

At one point my monthly pet insurance bill for six dogs, a cat and a pony (all of varying ages) was over £350 per month! However, we are just taking about one dog here for you, my beloved reader.

More on insurance in the Chapter 6.

Emergency Vet Bills

Totally your call if you get your dog insured or not but if you don't its certainly worth having a credit card with a high limit spare or a very healthy savings account for emergencies.

The treatments available to our pets now are amazing but also very costly.

Here are a few examples of average costs in the UK –

- Consultation fee £60 (this is just to see the vet, everything else is on top of this fee).
- Blood tests and X-rays are also pricey treatments, and you could be looking at a bill of between £100 and £130 for

blood tests, or as much as £300 for just one X-ray, often more than one is needed and this can be as much as an additional £100 per image.

- You may need to pay a supplement of up to £150 for out-of-hours emergency treatment – and if it involves an overnight stay at the practice, the bill could run to £500.
- The average cost of surgery is £1,500 and an ongoing treatment such as chemotherapy could come in at £5,000.
- CT scan up to £725
- Ultrasound Scan £45 – £150
- X-ray £235
- Endoscopy £495
- £1,860 MRI scan (out of hours/emergency £3025)

Figures are taken from moneysupermarket.com, animaltrust.org.uk & nimblefins.co.uk

Flea-ing/Worming (routine treatments)

While it is important that you follow veterinary recommendations for worming up to 6 months for a puppy to ensure they do not have a worm burden, it's also worth noting that there are alternatives to routine worming.

If you have horses, you may be familiar with the term 'faecal testing' this is where you send of a poo sample to be tested and then depending on the results only worm if the results come back positive. You can either have this done at your local vets or you can get this done through the many companies that provide this service. Google is your friend, though I tend to use a company called wormcount.com. There is also a herbal product called Verm- X that is useful for worming without chemicals.

I admit, I do not give my dogs anti-flea treatments regularly either. I try to keep my dogs as chemical free as possible. I rear my own dogs as holistically as is practical. Would I use a normal, chemical based flea treatment if they did contract fleas? Yes!

I use it as a cure rather than a prevention. Though there are a few supplements on the market that can help prevent fleas that are more natural solutions. A product called 'billy no mates' is just one of many. Generic flea treatments are insecticides, these are often applied topically to between their shoulder blades and we can be affected by this too when we stroke our dogs etc. As with all treatments there are risks and side effects. Some of which are very damaging.

There is also a trend for some fleas to be immune to certain brands or types of generic flea treatments too as they have been used as a prevention for so long (a little like antibiotic resistance in humans).

I am not your 'normal' dog owner, far from it! I look into everything and research and make my own decisions based upon that. My aim here is not to sway you either way, more highlight that just because the masses do something, that doesn't necessarily mean you should also. I'm highlighting that you have options and that if something doesn't feel or sound right to look into it more. Come to your own conclusions and make the best decisions for your dog.

Dog coats

Yes, most breeds of dog have their own built in coat, so why would they need us to buy them one?

Some breeds will suffer the cold more. Breeds such as Staffies and also Greyhounds and Whippets will benefit from wearing a coat for colder walks. Young puppies and also old dogs struggle to regulate their body temperature so coats can be helpful during these life stages too.

My own dogs are all long haired so shouldn't need coats, right? They don't NEED them; however, I need my dogs to have them to help reduce the daily mud battle with five throughout winter! They don't mind wearing them because they have all had coats since being puppies and it's easier to shove five coats in the wash than it is to hose or wash down 5 dogs after every winter walk. Call it lazy, call it what you will but that is what makes my life easier and ensures I have the time to get them out regularly in winter around my many other commitments.

I am talking about practical coats for dogs, not costumes or dressing the dogs up to look cute (though I have been there too in the past! Ziggy and Jazz had a better wardrobe than me at one point - yes, I'm rolling my eyes at this too don't worry!).

Quality dog coats will last wash after wash and winter after winter so invest wisely. I pay around £30 for a good quality Dachshund sized coat and paid around £75 for Merlin's coats (large Flatty, similar to the size of a Ridgeback). For Mica, our very small springer, her coats are normally around £40/45. Each of mine have at least two coats each, so I always have a spare if one is in the wash.

Extra washing

This is an easy one to overlook. Summer less so than winter but you will be washing dog beds, blankets, dog towels maybe toys and coats too. You will more than likely be out in the mud more than you were previous to getting a dog if this one is your first to so washing 'the dog walking coat & trousers' should be factored too.

A very difficult one to put a price on.

You may opt to buy a 'wash bag' to ensure the dog hair isn't going around and blocking your washing machine too, which is an additional cost to factor. These are normally orange in colour and are around £8-20 depending on what size you need.

Vehicle considerations

This may sound silly, but many overlook this aspect! Will your vehicle be big enough to transport your dog when it is fully grown and safely? Not only that but it is a legal requirement that your dog is restrained while traveling in your vehicle. I go into more detail about this in Chapter 7.

A seat belt harness, pet carrier, dog cage or dog guard are all acceptable and safe ways to transport your dog and all involve a financial cost to purchase.

I have some seatbelt harnesses which I found in the 'bargain bin' years ago and cost as little as £5-10 (keeping in mind if you opt for this option you are potentially putting a muddy pup on your seats in your care so a mud guard may be needed too and or frequent cleaning and valeting of your car).

You can purchase small soft/material crates from as little as £20 for small breeds, though the other end of the scale of this is bespoke make dog guards for your vehicle which can easily be in the £200-£2000 bracket!

Poo bags & disposal

Poo bags will be on your shopping list too, these can range from you using nappy sacks which are usually the cheapest choice (300 for 35p - Tesco Value) or to more expensive, heavy duty with tie handles and biodegradable (£5 for 100). A minor cost I'm sure you will agree but I'm also sure you are now seeing just how much expense having a puppy or dog can be and it all adds up!

For accidents around the house or deposits in the garden many people opt to flush it down the toilet, or to dispose of in their general household waste. This is of course your choice. It's worth also considering the amount of 'deposits' you will be disposing of, the bigger the dog the more it will be. Also, the lower quality food you feed will play a factor here - the amount of poo produced is higher, the lower quality food you feed.

You can purchase more eco-friendly options such as a 'poo wormery' which will degrade your pups' poo into compost.

When you are out and about in public it is of course a legal requirement to pick up your dog's poo. What many don't realise is that you can dispose of this in any public bin, not just a 'dog poo bin' though obviously I would advise that if there is a dog poo bin available to use this where possible. The waste from these bins are incinerated to reduce land fill when the contents of a generic public bin will head for land fill.

Treats

As a general guide you could be spending between £2-£10 per week on treats in the first year with puppy (if you are training lots, which you should be!)

Processed/dry versus smelly fresh treats:

Treats are, in my mind categorised in to two - General/Maintenance (around the house) and Training treats.

General maintenance treats are usually low value, dry processed treats. Examples would be just because we want to give them a treat and tell them how much of a good boy they are and how much we love them, for going to bed or for when we leave them for a period of time.

Dry treats are easy to use, less smelly and convenient in many cases. The cons to this is they are often more expensive than the other category and as they are dry may cause the dog to become more thirsty.

Training treats for more 'wages' for when we are training our puppy or dog a new skill or training them how to improve on something they already know. Ideally this should be something very smelly to the dog which means its normally more fresh food such as chicken, cheese, sausage etc. The fresh option is greasy on our hands etc but allows the dog to train for longer as they will work harder for something that is smelly and tasty and easily digestible.

Chews

As a general guide you could be spending between £2-£15 per week on chews in the first year with puppy.

Dogs need to chew, adults as well as puppies!

Kongs are, in my opinion THE best invention to keep dogs occupied, ever!

They are a rubber toy that has a hole through the middle that you can stuff with treats etc. You can also use these for play too as their shape means they bounce from the ground erratically which is exciting and keeps the interest of many dogs.

Kong stuffing is a great way to keep your pups or adult dog occupied and tired. Filling these with treats, their daily food, soft cheese, meat paste, banana etc and then placing in the freezer.

Giving frozen, stuffed Kongs to puppies and adult dogs makes the challenge harder, for it involves lots of licking and chewing to get at the tasty treats inside. This not only reduced mess but it also helps to sooth teething gums. I have included a Kong stuffing ideas and guide in your free bonuses which you can get either through my Facebook page or by emailing me - sarah@houndhelpers.co.uk

Other chews that in my opinion are great options are as follows;

Bulls Pizzles
Whimzees chews
Raw meaty bones (with care and research)
Beef hide (NOT rawhide)
Stag antlers
Empty hoof chews (not ready stuffed as these are often full of grit unfortunately)
Pigs ears (though these are fatty so in moderation)

Please avoid rawhide!

Rawhide chews are probably the most common chew and are widely available in pet shops. Unfortunately, I have yet to find a manufacturer of these which is still based in the UK. Most of these are now made in China and the ingredients commonly consist of leather, glue and dog… yes DOG! That doesn't sit well with me at all, as I'm sure it won't you either. Dogs cannot digest these chews and if fed enough times they will end up with an internal blockage which will mean a serious operation to remove it. Best to be avoided!

Other common chews that are best to avoid

This is due to less than desirable ingredients or the dog's inability to digest them:

Popular brand dental sticks
Coloured munchy rolls
Roast knuckle bones
Bones you have cooked (leftover from a roast maybe)
Any cooked bones

Cooked bones, Jazz's story

As I said at the start, I used to work in pet shops and would often bring home chews and toys for my dogs for when I was out at work (and if I'm really honest it was because I felt guilty about leaving them for so long). I often brought home the roast knuckle bones for my guys as they loved them, and they would last for so long. When Jazz was around a year of age I woke one morning, ready to get the dogs ready for an early walk before I headed off for a long day at work, I came into the kitchen to see my beautiful girl in her crate and sat in a pool of her own blood. Not a nice sight to wake up to, or see at any time. She was lethargic and after I checked her over, I could see the blood was coming from her back end. We rushed straight off to the vets, where she stayed for the day. I hated leaving her there and was so worried about her, I also had thoughts and fear of potentially losing her in my mind, especially after I had lost Rosco too. She spent the day at the vets, I was on the phone to them every hour to see what was going on and if she was ok. She had had X-rays and they had shown a shard of cooked bone had ripped her intestines as it was trying to pass through. An operation to remove the offending item and also the sew up her intestines followed and luckily my girl came home to me safe. A large vet bill and some carefully recovery protocols to go through along with painkillers, anti-inflammatory medications and strict instructions to not feed cooked bones again. I had more than learnt my lesson. These are a real danger to your dog's life; these bones were around the same size as her and yes, she still managed to break a piece off and ingest it.

Dogs cannot digest cooked bones. Best case, they will pass shards of it without issue, some will stay sat in the gut for years if not indefinitely and worst case they can cause death from internal bleeding or causing immovable blockages, please do not ever give your dogs any kind of cooked bone. Even if they are in pet shops this is no guarantee of safety! If you are buying bones from the pet shop and it's not stored in the freezer it is cooked - don't waste your money and put your dog's life at risk.

Chewing benefits for adult dogs as well as puppies

Dogs need to chew, ideally on appropriate items which you will know a bit more about by now. Chewing is a stress reliever, its mentally stimulating making the dog or puppy tired and it's also a pain reliever. Providing our dogs with things to chew throughout their lifetime is very beneficial just as much for us as it is for them.

Of course puppies have a need to chew that is greater than an adult due to teething (which lasts until around 6 months of age), but we shouldn't forget that adult dogs will enjoy a good chew and this also gives us a break too, particularly when they are going through their testing adolescent phase.

Holiday care

An expensive do. While many people rely on family and friends to care for their dog while they are away, what if they are also away or their circumstances change over your dog's life time? It is likely they will, we are talking about around 15 years - lots can change. You can never take a break away with these friends or family members without the dog if they are usually the ones to care for your dog.

Shopping list (example shopping list that I had for Ripple)

- Barriers such as a pen, crate, baby gates, etc.
- A heat mat /Snuggle safe heat pad /Hot water bottle wrapped in a towel
- Copious amounts of chews and activities
- Bedding, towels, bowls, grooming puppy brushes, toys etc.
- Travel/car crates etc.
- Puppy pads if required
- Collar, tag, harness and lead
- A new diary or notebook to put all your plans, goals, achievements, struggles and activities in for you to refer to.
- Plenty of memory on your camera/phone for all the lovely cute pictures you will be taking
- Ear plugs, energy (caffeine in my case), patience, maybe your alcoholic beverage of choice and a sense of humour!

Enrolling in a puppy class or private training help - worth its weight in gold for the right one! It is a cost that needs to be factored too. More on this in the next chapter.

Dog Food - a note on quality

Dogs are scavengers by nature so most will eat just about anything, that's not to say that something they enjoy is the best diet for them nor will it necessarily keep them healthy and in tip top condition. I enjoy a McDonalds; I probably have them more often than I should but if I ate these all the time, I would not be the healthiest.

Unfortunately, there are more low-quality dog foods on the market than there are good. Paying top prices doesn't necessarily mean the best either. This can be an absolute mine field. The best way to check the quality of a food brand is by checking through - https://www.allaboutdogfood.co.uk/

Unfortunately, the process in which dog food brands are passed for sale on supermarket shelves is not rigorous and brands merely have to prove that the food does not harm the dog over a three-month period. Three months out of a 15-year-old dog's lifetime is less than

1.7% of the dog's life! Many dogs are fed the same diet over their entire lifetime which can add to or cause both health and behavioural issues if not on the correct diet. Many dogs will develop allergies to the ingredients on their food is fed the same food for extend periods of time (years and years). This is another subject I really could go on and on about, but I will refrain for **I am not a canine nutritionist.** However, I will leave you with a few points to consider-

- Two of the most common and widely available brands of dog food are some of the absolute worst diets on the market. Please avoid. Many ingredients in these have been banned overseas. They are full of colourants, additives and preservatives that often cause serious health concerns and behaviour problems. Think in terms of blue smarties and E numbers for children.
- Most mainstream brands are owned by two major confectionary companies. Nestle - Bakers, Beta & Proplan to name but a few. Mars (as in Mars bars) own Pedigree, Chappie, James Wellbeloved & Royal Canin are amongst their many brands. These larger corporations can afford to pay for the space on supermarket shelves, the advertising and influencing people. Ensuring they become household names.
- Vets unfortunately do minimal study on canine nutrition when in training and the lectures they are provided with are mostly sponsored by the big brands so they are provided with biased and limited information which they pass on to pet owners unknowingly. Even many CPD courses I attend have been and are sponsored by these companies, offering free bags, pens, notepads etc. I hope you can start to see how they start to influence the professionals in the hope that they will recommend their brands.
- Most larger brands of dog food will have a 'breeder scheme' or club in which breeders are offered heavily discounted foods and products, knowing that many new puppy owners will be sent home with their brand of dog food and are more likely to continue feeding their brand, creating more sales for them in future.

Honestly there is much I could say, and absolutely horrify you with some of the ingredients in many dry dog foods as well as lower quality wet foods but the simplest way for you to check what foods are best is through the website that I have listed above. It would be helpful to you to check what food your breeder is feeding the puppies on. While each litter should be weaned onto a variety of foods and types to ensure a healthy gut with a varied diet a responsible breeder will send your puppy home with a week's supply of food that they have been using. I would definitely recommend keeping your puppy on this completely for at least 3 days to ensure they are settled into their new home with you before you start changing over the food if you choose to. If you choose to swap over their diet/food to another then please do this gradually, mixing the two to a greater and lesser extent over a five day period to ensure that the puppy does not react badly to a sudden change in diet, especially at such a crucial age and stage in their development.

I feed my own dogs on a raw meat, bones, veg and fruit diet - this is not practical for many and that is ok. As much as I am pro raw feeding, I also acknowledge there is yet to be a scientific study done to prove that this is in fact more beneficial over a dry food/kibble or wet food diet. However again the cynic in me says the raw food brands do not have the millions of £ or $ to fund these studies, and the larger corporations producing processed food do have the funding to either quash these studies or to produce biased studies to produce results in their favour. Many vets are against this style of feeding and will actively discourage pet owners to feed in this manner, instead often recommending a diet and brand that they sell in practice. All I can say is how much of a difference It has made to my own dogs over the last 8 years of feeding raw. Their coats are shinier they are calmer they have not had as many vets' visits.

I'll say it again, I am NOT a canine nutritionist and I could have in fact been fed and chose to believe biased data – please do your own research on this.

If you do decide to look at raw feeding, please do your research as done wrong this is very harmful too. Use the all about dog food website and do your own research, come to your own conclusions and make the best choice not only for your dog but for your lifestyle and budget too.

I used to feed my own dogs Proplan dry food for many years as that's what Rosco and Ziggy's breeder had sent them both home with. They seemed to do well on it, so why change it was my thinking. I know now that their breeder was on their breeder scheme and the clever marketing had worked! It wasn't until Merlin joined us and didn't get on with any kind of dry food (he loved it but the puddles that came out of the other end said otherwise), no matter what dry food I tried his deposits were still far from firm. This led me to research alternative types of food and I learnt a lot about the power of influence and some of the disgusting ingredients in the foods that are so widely available.

Puppy Prepared?

5 PET CARE PROFESSIONALS AND SERVICES - A WORD OF WARNING

Dog walkers, trainers, pet sitters, kennels, day care establishments, home boarders and groomers - none of these industries are regulated.

Seriously! There is no governing body to ensure that they adhere to a minimum standard of care, knowledge or experience.

There are slightly more rules for home boarders, day care establishments and kennels to adhere to with the recent addition to the licensing laws for these professional services. Firstly - check if they are licensed and to what level, you will be able to find this information on their local council website.

In 12 years of business there is one thing that still saddens me and has done from the start.

Yes, I provide many of the services listed above or have done in the past if not now.

What saddens me about this industry is that it remains to this day, unregulated. This is not just dog walkers, it applies to trainers, groomers, day care establishments and much more. There has been talk of regulating it for years, but it is just that - talk. We are caring for your precious family members and in the wrong hands it can, and often does end in disaster. This then paints the rest of us with the same brush. Over the past five years I have noticed many, many people start up as a dog walking enterprise and while some will stick at it and do good things, the majority either give up or worse they do not educate themselves in dog language, the law and dog management and make mistakes. We are all human and we all make mistakes but not ensuring you are knowledgeable in your field is ignorance and, in some cases, arrogant.

The last 12 months has seen us welcome a higher percentage of clients and dogs into our walks who have previously used another dog walking provider. We have then spent months trying to improve the dog's behaviour that has been caused by the previous service provider. What's sadder is this isn't just one company that these dogs are coming to us from. We love to help these hounds and their owners, we rejoice in seeing the results and hearing from the owners what a difference it has made. However, the point is, we shouldn't have to fix the issues in the first place. Often the owners don't even realise what has happened, they just see a deterioration in their dog's happiness and behaviour.

Just because someone is insured and CRB checked that does not mean they are 'qualified' to care for your dog in any capacity'.

Dogs die in the care of so-called professionals every day. They are beaten, hit and kicked behind closed doors. And their behaviour can deteriorate from a simple lack of skills and knowledge on the pet care providers part. I don't mean to scare you with this, but it is worth being very aware of this. After-all, you have spent the time and money in investing in this book, so you want to get it right from the start. Substandard care can quickly undo all of your hard work.

Most pet owners will need to use a pet care provider at some point over their pet's lifetime, please do your research, get to know them before handing over your precious family member.

The link to the professional dog walking guidelines that have been published is in the links and resources section. Or you can google Professional dog walker guidelines UK.

They are not hard fast rules, as I said before this is not regulated but it is something you should be looking at when employing a pet carer and questioning if they adhere to these guidelines. They may not be aware of them, but you can ask how they do certain things or don't do certain things using the guide as an outline for when you quiz them.

Dog trainers and behaviourists

Again, sadly no regulation. There are hundreds if not thousands of membership schemes and organisations that portray themselves to be governing bodies that professionals can join. If you see that the trainer you are looking at is affiliated with an organisation, usually this is letters, an acronym either after their name or stated on their website. Then check out the organisation, their own website. Look at their code of practice that your trainer has signed up to and what the process is to become accredited with them, if they are in fact accredited and not just a student member and if their beliefs in training are aligned with your own. For practice check out who I am with - the KCAI (kennel club accredited instructor) and QIDTI (qualified international dog training instructor).

If nothing else do your research, ask for recommendations, look for reviews online etc.

Dog training classes

It has now been proven that taking your puppy to puppy training classes are beneficial to your dog's overall behaviour throughout its lifetime (I have to add, that the right class is key here).

Taking your puppy along to classes may cost more than a walk in the park or a run along the beach, but researchers have revealed that it helps to make them more confident animals in their adult life.

The study found that those pups who were taken to six weekly classes were able to cope better with strangers, grew up better behaved and were less stressed.

Picking the right classes for you and your puppy is important. Go and watch a class first without your puppy. Watch who the trainers help, is it the best dogs that they spend more time with or the ones who need the help the most? How many dogs are in the class and how many trainers are there, what's the ratio? A small numbers class with more than one trainer is ideal.

Are the trainers offering/teaching more than one way to do things? If they only know one way to teach something this isn't a sign of a knowledgeable trainer.

Do you like the trainer? If you don't like them then you are not likely to pay attention and learn much from them. A little like we always do better at school in the classes and subject shower we like the teacher.

If a class or training club does not want you to come and watch first then they are not worth wasting your time and money on.

Often the best classes are fully booked in advance so you may need to do this research before puppy comes home to ensure you can get on the list and get to classes at the right time.

Puppy Parties

Vets will often offer puppy parties; these are rarely a good thing for your puppy. My best advice is to avoid like the plague!

The promise of these events is that you can take your puppy to socialise with other puppies while they wait to be allowed out after vaccinations are complete (I will share more to do with vaccinations and socialisation) and get a good experience at the vets. In reality most cases the puppies learn only to be bullied or how to be a bully to others and this is a pattern that is then set for life. Unfortunately, most vets puppy parties are primarily run by inexperienced veterinary nurses who may have only attended a one or two day course on puppies and training. Puppies do not need to interact with other puppies and in reality, you are not only paying for your puppy to learn bad habits but you are also giving up your time for a long sales pitch on neutering, fleeing and worming treatments etc. Vets and veterinary nurses are very well educated in animal illnesses, symptoms, treatments and medications they are not well educated in training and behaviour.

Puppy Prepared?

6 HEALTH ISSUES

Breed specific concerns, testing etc.

If you are looking at a pedigree or a cross breed this is just as important. Many of the fashionable and common crosses of breeds suffer the same health problems in both breeds so the parents should still be health tested.

The Kennel Club website will be able to tell you what tests they advise for each breed, so if you are unsure have a look there. I can't list each breed and each health issue here for two reasons, one it would be very boring as you would be scouring the many pages just to look for the few breeds you are interested in, discarding the rest and two this book would be more like a compendium than a handbook!

Back to cross breeds - one of, if not the most common cross breed in the UK at the moment is the Cockerpoo - a mix between a cocker spaniel and a poodle. Both of these breeds suffer from an eye problem called PRA which means both parents should be tested, even when crossing breeds.

PRA (progressive retinal atrophy)

If a pup is affected by PRA once it becomes an adult from a fairly young age they will start with symptoms, such as not being able to see in the dark or in low light which progresses on to total blindness. This then encourages the growth of cataracts which in themselves do not cause an issue if there is no sight but then progressing onto glaucoma, pressure in the eye which causes pain and often dogs will need to have their eyes removed in cases such as these. For PRA there is a simple genetic test, a swab of saliva and cheek cells taken from the mouth and sent off to the Animal Health Trust (AHT) with a fee to be analysed. There are three possible outcomes for this test - clear, carrier or affected.

Clear - the dog is clear from the genetic marker for this disease, will never be affected by it.
Carrier - despite the seemingly negative label this is also safe, the dog simply carries the marker for the disease but it lays dormant, the dog will never suffer from PRA. But if the dog is to be bred from it should only be mated with a clear.
Affected - the dog will be affected by the disease.

Unless you are planning to breed from your puppy in future you will have no need to have your dog tested if the parents have been responsibly bred and have desirable results to the tests.

There is a fourth category here but a test isn't necessarily needed - the parents if KC registered the puppy may be listed as **'hereditary clear'** this means both of their parents were tested and have a clear test result. Puppies from a clear to clear mating will be automatically categorised as clear from the disease.

Conversely if your pup is either labeled as a carrier or is likely to be a carrier do not let this put you off the puppy, your puppy will never ever suffer from this disease.

Ziggy, my own boy is affected by PRA. We were lucky in the respect that he wasn't affected till his later years, his eyesight started to deteriorate at around 10 years of age and even now at 14 he can still see in daylight, albeit a little hazy. Most dogs affected by this are totally blind by the age of 5!

Allergies

In my view this is becoming an absolute epidemic in dogs as I would say over half the dogs I work with have an allergy of some form or another and in varying degrees. My first larger dog Bella (who was essentially a mongrel, made up of 5 different breeds of varying degrees and percentages) suffered greatly with many types of environmental allergies, including an allergy to grass and pollen! Our older Springer girl Mica has allergies too. There is little worse than watching your dog be uncomfortable and constantly scratching at themselves.

Veterinary treatments are progressing all the time and new treatments being developed to help alleviate the symptoms, but we should obviously be trying to avoid purchasing a dog with allergies at all costs to start with.

Allergies are related to the strength and development of the immune system and the immune system is largely controlled by gut health. A litter of puppies with a very varied diet once weaned can certainly help you avoid having a dog with allergies. A puppy from parents who do not have allergies and also a puppy that is bred from a bitch that has not had a stressful pregnancy. (More on stress during pregnancy and lactation later). Stress also affects the immune system, the same as with humans, if we are going through a period of stress our immune system lacks the ability to fight off colds and viruses as well as when we are not stressed.

Cancer

Cancer in dogs is more and more common nowadays, another thing related to the immune systems strength and robustness. In certain breeds cancer is the biggest killer. Particularly in Flatcoat retrievers its very common for cancer to take hold and cause death between the young ages of 6 and 8 - way too young I'm sure you will agree. In Boxers, and Golden Retrievers cancer is also a massive issue and worry. There are many theories for the causes of cancer some being over vaccination (refer to chapter 13) some being genetics plus many more theories. My opinion is it's all of the above, over breeding (closely related matings, smaller gene pools) the increased use of chemicals in dogs foods, vaccinations, flea and worming treatments and the chemicals we use on a daily basis in the house for cleaning and such like, but hey I'm no vet, scientist nor geneticist.

Cruciate ligament disease

The cruciate ligaments sit inside the knee joint, holding it together. They are bands of tough fibrous tissue that connect the thigh bone (femur), to the shin bone (tibia).

In the vast majority dogs, the cruciate ligament ruptures as a result of long-term degeneration, the fibres within the ligament weaken over time, like a fraying rope. The cause of this is not known, but genetic factors are probably most important, with certain breeds being predisposed (including Labradors, Rottweilers, Boxers, West Highland White Terriers and Newfoundlands). Other factors such as obesity, individual conformation, hormonal imbalance and certain inflammatory conditions of the joint may also play a role.

Limping is the commonest sign of cruciate injury. This may appear suddenly during or after exercise in some dogs, or it may be progressive and intermittent in others. Some dogs are affected in both knees at the same time, and these dogs often find it difficult to rise from a down position and have a very wobbly gait. In severe cases, dogs cannot get up at all and can be suspected of having a neurological problem.

Cruciate disease is diagnosed by feeling for abnormal movement in the knee joint. X-rays or MRI scans can also be required. An exploratory arthroscopy (keyhole surgery) can be used to confirm the diagnosis and to investigate for possible cartilage tears or other problems.

Treatment usually involves surgery but there is a non-surgical management method.
Non-surgical treatment methods involve body weight management, physiotherapy, exercise modification and medication (anti-inflammatory painkillers). Dogs greater than 15kg have a very poor

chance of becoming clinically normal with non-surgical treatment. Dogs weighing less than 15kg have a better chance, although improvement usually takes several months and is rarely complete.

Treatment without surgery relies on the dog building extra strength around the knee joint which takes the strain off the broken cruciate ligament. Their pain has to be managed in the meantime. Recovery can take months and the aim is for your dog not to be in pain in the long term. Even with successful treatment some dogs might still walk with a slight limp but hopefully no pain.

There are several surgical options that aim to replace the damaged ligament and those that render the ligament redundant by cutting the tibia and re-aligning the forces acting within the knee joint.

Post-surgery the recovery period involves the same processes as the non-surgical treatment option but hopefully with a better long-term outlook.

Hip Dysplasia

The hips are 'ball and socket' joints, which normally fit together perfectly to enable easy movement. Hip dysplasia is when the hip joints don't fit together properly and become unstable. Hip dysplasia causes pain, swelling, stiffness and eventually arthritis.

Dogs with hip dysplasia usually begin showing symptoms while they are growing (at around 5-6 months of age). The condition tends to be worse in medium - large breed dogs, fast growing dogs, overweight dogs and dogs who have been over-exercised when young.

Dogs with hip dysplasia also develop a wobbly or swaying walk and a "bunny hop" when running with both back legs moving together. They find it difficult to jump and to go up and down stairs. Their hips also become quite skinny due to the small weakened muscles in the back legs and hips

Initial treatment is body weight management, physiotherapy,

exercise modification and medication (anti-inflammatory painkillers). There are a number of surgical options available which can be offered depending on the severity of the disease which modify the hip anatomy.

The symptoms of hip dysplasia often continue throughout a dog's life, so requiring ongoing care and treatment. This can be physiotherapy or hydrotherapy and often joint supplements are suggested to slow down the deterioration of the arthritis.

Any breed of dog can develop hip dysplasia, but it is much more common in medium to large breed pedigrees including Labrador, German Shepherd, Golden Retriever, Rottweiler, Bernese Mountain Dog, and Newfoundland.

The best ways to prevent hip dysplasia is to stop breeding from dogs with the condition and also environmental factors are very important.

Although there is a genetic influence on hip dysplasia, the heritability of the trait is rather low. Ensuring no injury or strain on the joints when puppy is young, with things like ensuring non slip flooring etc is a big factor in the road to prevention.

Screening programs are available to check that your dog has healthy hips, and if choosing to buy a breed prone to hip dysplasia, check that both parents have been hip scored and are below the breed average. You can find the breeds average score on the KC website or the breed council/club website.

Elbow Dysplasia

Elbow dysplasia is a painful condition that causes one or both elbows to develop abnormally while a puppy is growing. There are three main areas inside the elbow joint that can be affected; some dogs have just one problem area, while others suffer with a combination. Most dogs have a limp on one or both front legs. Elbow dysplasia is the most common cause of forelimb lameness in young, large and giant breed dogs

Most dogs start showing symptoms between 5 - 18 months old of lameness, stiffness, sometimes swelling around the elbow and the front paws can begin to point outwards and/or the elbows are held at a strange angle. These factors lead onto arthritis.

Elbow dysplasia is most common in medium to large breed dogs, including; Labrador, Golden Retriever, Rottweiler, German Shepherd, Bernese Mountain Dogs, Newfoundland and Bassett Hound.

This condition is primarily of genetic cause although environmental factors, such as obesity during puppyhood, may influence whether an animal with the genes will develop a clinical problem. Diagnosis involves X-rays leading onto CT or MRI scans and an elbow arthroscopy

Surgical treatments for elbow dysplasia aim to treat the current source of pain and also to minimise the likelihood of osteoarthritis progression. Non-surgical treatments for elbow dysplasia aim to treat elbow pain and maintain mobility but do not have the potential to minimise osteoarthritis progression. Non-surgical treatment involves body weight management, physiotherapy, exercise modification and medication (anti-inflammatory painkillers).

Much the same as hip dysplasia a test/elbow scoring should be done on the parents, aiming for a combined score below the breed average.

Luxating Patella

The patella is a small bone at the front of the knee (stifle joint). In humans we refer to it as the 'knee-cap'. It is positioned between the quadriceps muscle and a tendon that attaches to the shin bone (tibia). The patella glides in a groove at the end of the thigh bone (femur) as the knee flexes and extends. Occasionally the patella slips out of the groove. This is called luxation, or dislocation, of the patella which then means that the knee cannot properly extend.

This is a common condition and is more common in smaller dogs (although dogs of all sizes can be affected). Most dogs will show signs as puppies or young adults, although onset of signs in mature dogs is also common. Dogs with a "bow-legged" stance are more likely to be affected by patellar luxation. A characteristic "skipping" lameness is often seen, where the dog will limp for a few steps and then quickly return to normal, but some dogs will limp continuously. Dogs affected by patellar luxation in both knees will have a stiff, awkward gait with knees that do not extend properly.

The condition is primarily of genetic cause and is the consequence of the selective breeding of dogs with a preferred (bow-legged) conformation. The dog is born with normal knees but begins to develop abnormalities of the bones and muscles of the hind limbs early in life.

Patellar luxation is most common in certain breeds of dogs, such as Poodles, Yorkshire Terriers, Staffordshire Bull Terriers and Labrador Retrievers. Luxation of the patella due to injury (trauma) is uncommon.

This condition is diagnosed by physical examination and the severity is graded by how mobile the "knee-cap" is. There is non-surgical management and surgical options. The luxating patella maybe mild but can then cause other conditions on other joints as abnormal stresses are put on the limb. It will also likely lead to osteoarthritis of the knee joint.

The outlook with patellar luxation surgery is generally good. Although dogs develop osteoarthritis to some degree, this is often not a cause of pain or lameness.

Epilepsy

Epilepsy is a chronic condition that causes repeated seizures (fits or funny turns). Seizures are the physical manifestation of uncontrolled electrical activity in the brain and are the most common neurological problem in dogs. According to the KC approximately 1 in 130 dogs in the UK are affected.

The abnormal electrical activity leads to sudden but short-lived changes in the dog's behaviour and/or movements. There are 2 types of seizures in dogs: "partial" seizures that involve more focal areas of the brain and may appear as muscle spasms/tremors or where the dog may just look dazed and unsteady. More commonly 'generalised' seizures are seen where the dog will often collapse onto their side and make jerking movements with their legs, and they may go rigid. The dog can foam at the mouth and may also lose control of their bladder or bowel at the same time. During this time the dog is unconscious with most seizures lasting between one and three minutes. Afterwards some dogs will get back onto their paws and carry on as normal straight away, while others can remain dazed for up to 24 hours.

There is no diagnostic test for epilepsy, but a series of tests can be performed to rule out other causes for the seizures including taking blood and urine samples and possibly an MRI scan.

Treatment is with anti-epileptic drugs that aim to increase quality of life by reducing the frequency and severity of the seizures. There will also be the need for regular reviews with the vet to assess the effectiveness of the drug used and to monitor the liver and renal function of the dog.

Ziggy also suffers with Epilepsy, and this will shorten his lifespan. It's not nice to watch your dog suffer and while this sent always down to genetics its worth keeping in mind. If you find your dog having a fit, try to keep calm, dim the lights if possible and time how long the fit lasts for to then report to your vet (maybe even video the fit so you can show your vet, though this is hard in that moment of panic).

Heart Disease & Heart Problems

Approximately 15% of UK dogs will suffer from some kind of heart condition during their life. The most common condition being heart failure which will be caused by a secondary problem. This secondary condition can be due to congenital heart defects (present from birth) or acquired (disease that develops over time). Some of the congenital conditions appear to be hereditary (passed on from parents to offspring) and are found in certain breeds of dog. Ageing is the most common reason dogs develop heart conditions, but obese dogs are more susceptible.

Symptoms that you may see in a dog with a heart condition involve tiredness, lethargy, breathing difficulties that include shortness of breath, frequent coughing that can lead to gagging, reduced appetite and/or noticeable weight gain or loss, abdominal swelling. The dog may also experience fainting or collapsing. It is important to note however that early on there may be no symptoms at all.

A vet will be able to diagnose a heart condition by clinical examination X-rays, heart tracings (ECG) and cardiac ultrasound scans. Blood and urine tests will also provide useful information and then the correct course of treatment can be started. So routine visits to the vet can help catch heart disease while it is asymptomatic.

Although heart conditions in dogs cannot be prevented with the exception of heartworm disease, the goal is always early diagnosis and treatment. This involves medications that manage and slow down the progression of the disease which can improve quality of life and extend life expectancy.

Chronic valvular disease is more common in small breeds such as Miniature Poodles, Cocker Spaniels, Pomeranians and Schnauzers. Myocardial disease is more common in large and giant breeds like Great Danes and Irish Wolfhounds.

Ziggy, amongst his many health issues also has a heart murmur, he is currently grade 3, but he is doing well at present without medication. A heart murmur can also be temporary and brought on by high stress. I have known a few female dogs develop a heart murmur through a stressful birth or from a large litter to find that six to twelve months later the heart murmur has gone or at least lessened.

Insurance, Vet monthly clubs & Subscriptions

I have noticed an increase of the monthly subscriptions to veterinary practices. These are often for under £20 per month and offer benefits such as reduced vet fees, fleeing worming treatments, vaccinations etc. Me being the sceptic that I am I would advise against these (especially now you are more aware of the facts about 'routine treatments'). The vets would not be offering these subscriptions if they were not making money from them, now would they? Using minimal treatments only when needed is not only creating a healthier dog for you but it's also saving your bank balance. I understand the mentality that people have when they do sign up for these schemes – it's a set amount that is paid each month to reduce the big shock bills we get when we could really do without them, but then again I know I personally would rather save money over time than to pay out more monthly over the same period. I have signed up to these in the past but many many years ago, when I wasn't aware of the regulations and the potential harm I was causing to my dogs, by giving them monthly topical treatments and yearly vaccinations when they are not needed.

Ongoing health issues for pet dogs is now very common and affects over 60% of dogs! (Research by The Leadership Factor 2017). This means you have more chance of having a dog who needs regular treatments throughout their lifetime than having one that is healthy and hardly ever needs to visit the vets. Our dogs become family and its awful to see them suffer, a lack of funds to provide current treatment should not be an issue if you have planned ahead and catered for emergencies.

If you decide to insure your dog please ensure you have a lifetime or maximum benefit policy. This essentially means that as long as you keep up the policy then the insurance will pay for medical costs that carry over from one policy year to the next without issue, though you often will be expected to pay your excess for each year when claiming (an excess for each separate issue). Make sure you check how much your pet is covered for for each year, in this day and age is you have a breed who is predisposed to problems the basic £4k a year just isn't enough. Up until recently all six of my dogs and my cat and my pony were all insured and yes, the total 'pet insurance' bill each month was effectively equivalent to a second mortgage.

Recently we opted to cancel Merlin, Ziggy and Dobi's policies, but this is only because of their old age and slower rate of recovery from major illnesses or injuries - considering if it would be fair to fix a broken leg when the dog is 14 years of age which could take 6,8 or 10 months to heal which could be spent in a crate, on restricted movement and in some amount of pain even with pain killers. Hubby and I discussed this at length, we both said if anything happened to any of these three, we would not put them through any operations, X-rays or procedures as they wouldn't cope with it and it wouldn't be fair at their age. Of course if they needed a course of painkillers or medication to make them more comfortable we would pay this out of our own pocket (which essentially would be around the same cost as the policy excess anyway) if it was anything more serious it wouldn't be fair to put them through it and instead would opt for euthanasia. Not something we take likely but knowing our pets this would be the kindest thing to do for them and euthanasia often is not covered under the insurance anyway.

As I mentioned before Merlin had health issues since he was 3 years of age, and our insurance policy paid out over £20k over the years, which is at least three times the value of the payments I have made for the policy.

One year he was very ill, and we had maxed out his £4k allowance on the policy within the first 6 months of that policy year. This meant that we had to pay for the remainder of his treatment our of our own pockets - in excess of £150 a week for 6 months! It wasn't easy but we were still glad to have had insurance and this just is one reason I say that 4k per year per issue just isn't enough. I should add also that the £150 per week was after I shopped around and got the medications online after paying for a written prescription form the vets. If I had purchased the medications direct from my vets it would have been almost double the amount per week. We had a wonderfully happy and bouncy further three years with Merlin after he had finished this period of medications and issues before his passing in March 2019.

Do your homework with your insurance, don't just go for the cheapest, look at the reviews, speak to your vets if they have had any issues with a company paying out. Larger more popular insurance companies are rarely the cheapest but the vets will often do what is called a 'direct claim' with them meaning you only have to pay the excess amount and they will claim for the remaining balance direct from the insurance company meaning you don't have to make the payment in full and wait for the insurance to pay you back. A company I have used for almost 15 years is VIP (Vet Insurance Protector) they are a broker, but you do not get charged for using the service. They are a small company and will help you find the best policy for your needs at the best price and answer any questions you have truthfully. You can even call them for claim forms or to make any changes to the policy which saves you being on hold to the insurance company for wasting your valuable time each time you have a question.

Congenital issues and pre-existing conditions

Some dogs unfortunately are born with health problems. Some maybe born malformed, blind, with cataracts, a club foot or with some other defect. I implore you not to buy this puppy as tempting as it may be as you want to take care of it. Sometimes even the best of breeders will produce this kind of puppy, its the way nature works but it should not be your job to take this puppy home no matter how tempting it may be.

You can also have issues getting this dog insured for this issue that it suffers from or anything relating to it as it is classes as a 'pre-existing issue'.

As I said in the costings chapter that as the years progress insurance premiums can creep up. Whether from age or from previous claims or both it can become very expensive. If you are changing companies and have made a claim for something in the past you should expect to find that this issue will not be covered in future with another company as it is a 'pre-existing condition' and as such excluded from cover. It's very similar in health insurance in humans. There may come a point that you decide to stop insuring your dog and have a credit card on hand for emergencies (but please do not forget to ensure you have public liability cover if you decide to do this).

Complementary therapies

Did you know that there are massage therapists and chiropractors for dogs?

There are countless types of complementary therapies available to dogs and some of which can be key in rehabilitation after injury, surgery or when dealing with an ongoing health issue.

I have used the following therapies for my own dogs -

- Hydrotherapy
- Acupuncture
- Massage (specifically Galen Therapy)
- Zoopharmacognosy
- Chiropractic care
- Reiki
- Lazer therapy

This is by no means a comprehensive list of therapies that are available, but maybe the most popular ones.

If you have insurance for your dog and have complementary therapy cover you can use this to pay for such things (after you have paid the excess required) provided it is by recommendation from the vet and the practitioner you are using is recognised with a governing body that is also recognised by your insurance company.

7 THE LAW & YOUR RESPONSIBILITIES IF LIVING IN THE UK

Some may surprise you so please do not skip what you may think is a boring chapter.

The five freedoms

Animal Welfare Act 2006 introduced an essential concept for pet owners and those responsible for domestic animals, e.g., breeders, those who have working animals or farm animals in England and Wales.

Preventing animals suffering: If this advice is not followed or the animal's needs are not being met, then action can be taken whether through a formal warning or in some cases a prosecution.

What does the law actually say?
Section 9 of the Animal Welfare Act places a duty of care on people to ensure they take reasonable steps in all the circumstances to meet the welfare needs of their animals to the extent required by good practice.

What does this mean for those responsible for animals?

In short it means they must take positive steps to ensure they care for their animals properly and in particular must provide for the five welfare needs, which are:

1. Need for a suitable environment.
2. Need for a suitable diet.
3. Need to be able to exhibit normal behaviour patterns.
4. Need to be housed with, or apart, from other animals.
5. Need to be protected from pain, suffering, injury, and disease.

The Law

The Law and Dogs in the UK is continually changing, and not in favour of us multidog owners. Many councils now have enforced local bylaws that in public parks only four dogs per person are allowed (regardless of size, obedience or if on or off lead), this is worth considering if you are getting number 5 or above. Or if you plan to travel within the UK with your dogs on holiday as your holiday destination may have this rule in place. The fact is the more dogs you have, the more likely they are to cause a nuisance, or noise disturbance when someone rings the doorbell, two dogs barking are louder than one, and yes, I admit it I cringe when our doorbell goes as it sounds like I have 20 dogs, not 6!

The law applies to all breeds of dogs

It's against the law to let a dog be dangerously out of control anywhere, such as:

- In a public place.
- In a private place, e.g., a neighbour's house or garden.
- In the owner's home.

Some types of dogs are banned.

Your dog is considered dangerously out of control if it:

- Injures someone.

- Makes someone worried that it might injure them.

A court could also decide that your dog is dangerously out of control if any of the following apply:

- It attacks someone's animal.
- The owner of an animal thinks they could be injured if they tried to stop your dog from attacking their animal.
- A farmer is allowed to kill your dog if it's worrying livestock.

Penalties

You can get an unlimited fine or be sent to prison for up to 6 months (or both) if your dog is dangerously out of control. You may not be allowed to own a dog in the future, and your dog may be destroyed.

If you let your dog injure someone you can be sent to prison for up to 5 years or fined (or both). If you deliberately use your dog to injure, someone, you could be charged with 'malicious wounding'.

If you allow your dog to kill someone you can be sent to prison for up to 14 years or get an unlimited fine (or both).

If you allow your dog to injure an assistance dog (e.g., a guide dog), you can be sent to prison for up to 3 years or fined (or both).

The laws that apply to the above, of which you can be prosecuted under are - The Dangerous dogs act and the Control of dogs act. These laws apply to ALL dogs, not just the banned breeds

Dog Breeding Licences

As of October 2018, new breeding regulations were introduced in England by Defra and the Kennel Club is providing information to its customers on how some of these changes will effect dog breeders and some of those involved with dogs.

The main legislative changes being made are:

- A breeding licence will be required for anyone breeding three or more litters and selling at least one puppy in a 12-month period. This is a reduction from the previous litter test of five or more litters.
- A licence is not required if documentary evidence can be provided that none of the puppies or adult dogs have been sold.
- Anyone in the business of selling dogs (even one or two litters in a 12-month period) may require a licence. This is not new and has been in place since 1999. The Government provides guidance on what local authority inspectors should consider when assessing whether a breeder meets the business test.
- A new star rating system is being introduced based on welfare conditions and breeding history which has been designed to reward high performing breeding establishments and to give further help to puppy buying public in identifying good breeders.

You can check if your breeder has a licence by contacting their local council licensing department.

Dog home boarding licences

There have been changes to this also. The changes came into place in October 2018. Essentially anyone who is running a pet care business or earning over £1000 per year from caring for other people's dogs in their own home or on their own property are required to have a licence to do so. *this currently only affects England

Noise complaints

While dogs are allowed to bark, they are not allowed to bark so that it causes a nuisance. It is a matter of fact, and the degree in each case and factors that may be taken into account include the volume, duration of the barking and the time of day it happens. The test is whether it is of a nature which makes it intrusive or irritating.

If a complaint is made to a local Council, they have a duty to investigate. The Council may serve a Noise Abatement Notice, and if the barking continues then, they may prosecute under the Environmental Protection Act 1990. The likely penalty is a fine.

The neighbour may also take civil action.

Please note that the above summary only relates to the law in England and Wales. You must not rely on it as constituting legal advice, and so for specific guidance on your particular dog law issue I would recommend visiting doglaw.co.uk or contacting Trevor Cooper at Trevor Cooper and co dog law solicitors.

Identification (ID)

In the UK, the Control of Dogs Order 1992 states that any dog in a public place must wear a collar with the name and address (including postcode) of the owner engraved or written on it or engraved on a tag.

Failure to do so can incur a fine of up to £5000! Please note that the ID should be on the collar, so if your dog is only walked on a harness, a collar and tag/ID should still be worn.

A public place also covers when your dog is in your vehicle.

Exceptions to identification laws apply to working dogs only when they are actually working and for assistance dogs.

It's also worth noting that if you let others walk or take your dog off your property without correct ID and they are caught that person or persons will be liable to pay the fine.

Contrary to popular belief, the ID rules are not in place for us to get our dogs back if they are lost. Yes, it serves this purpose too, but the rules are in place for liability. If your dog causes an accident, you or the person in charge of the dog at the time is liable for any damage. Most pet insurance policies cover you for public liability, as do some home insurance policies. If in doubt check! Failing that, the Dogs Trust offer a yearly membership for £25 which will cover you for instances such at this.

Microchipping

All owners must ensure their dog is microchipped and their details are kept up to date. Not only will this mean the UK's 8.5 million dogs can be returned to their owners more quickly if they wander too far from home, but it will also make it easier to track down the owners of dogs that carry out attacks on people.

Breeders must now have puppies microchipped by the age of 8 weeks (before leaving for new homes).

Check which company your pup's chip is registered with and that the vet can scan the chip when you visit. Some foreign manufacturers are causing issues with registrations in the UK. Chips not being able to be read or be registered resulting in dogs not being traced back to their owners.

Travel in Vehicles

It's estimated that one third of UK drivers are not complying with the law when it comes to restraining their dog in the car whilst driving, and are risking a fine of up to £2,500, according to recent research. These drivers are also putting their pets' lives and themselves at risk.

Rule 57 of the Highway Code states: "When in a vehicle make sure dogs or other animals are suitably restrained so they cannot distract you while you are driving or injure you, or themselves, if you stop quickly. A seat belt harness, pet carrier, dog cage or dog guard are ways of restraining animals in cars."

Alarmingly, the research states that 34% of drivers fail to restrain pet passengers, 1 in 10 allow their pets to sit in the front seat of the car, while a further 9% of drivers allow their pet to sit on the back seat without a harness.

The research, carried out by Confused.com, shows that 64% of drivers are unaware that having an unrestrained pet passenger is punishable with a fine. Drivers who fail to restrain their pets whilst driving may also be incriminating themselves by driving without proper control of a motor vehicle or driving without due care and attention.

Risking lives & invalidating your insurance

If you should have an accident or have to make a sudden stop, an unrestrained pet could be thrown forward and injure themselves and potentially injure you or other passengers.

Furthermore, car insurance providers reserve the right to invalidate policies if a driver is involved in an accident with an unrestrained pet. Confused.com's research shows that 10% of drivers involved in an accident would result in having their policy invalidated.

Puppy Prepared?

8 COI % WHAT IS IT AND HOW DO WE USE IT?

Coefficient Of Inbreeding - a measurement of degree of inbreeding

What the hell does that mean?

This is the percentage of which you dog has the same ancestors on both sides of its family, both mother and father. The number of dogs that are related to each other on both sides, the amount your dog has the same genetic makeup or how much is it 'inbred'

No pedigree will be 0% … the process in which you create a breed is to breed similar dogs together, from similar lines so you get a number of dogs looking the same or vastly similar, this means all dogs of the same breed are at some point related, just as we are to a certain respect to all other humans, many many generations back we have shared ancestors.

The rarer the breed you choose the smaller the gene pool will be, the fewer dogs that can be used for breeding and such the percentage of COI will be higher. The higher the COI the more likely that health problems, or behaviour problems will occur.

Each breed has an average COI score which changes from year to year. You can check your breeds average on the mykc.org website. Ideally you should be looking for a puppy that is equal to or below the breed average for your best chances of success. How do you find out what your puppy will be?

If they are KC registered you can visit the website and type in the registered name of the mother or father of your puppy and see what their individual COI is, then click on 'hypothetical mating' and enter the fathers registered name, this will then calculate the COI for your puppy. This is particularly useful if the puppies have yet to be registered or even born. If they have already been registered, then you can type in any of the puppies registered names from the litter and it will give you the calculation.

The KC do not allow puppies to be registered from mother to son, daughter to father or brother to sister matings now which helps to keep this score down and discourage the practice. They will however allow this practice and register puppies in extenuating circumstances, but this is rare and likely not the puppy you will be wanting anyway.

This is also one of the reasons I personally like to have a KC registered dog if I'm going for a pedigree. There are no guarantees by any means by having a registered pedigree but as you can see it provides you with more information and peace of mind than one that isn't. Never mind the ethical concerns of how many litters can be bred from a bitch, the KC limit breeders to four litters before the age of 8 for any bitch.

Breeding from your dog in future?

I hope you are starting to see as you progress through the book just how much can go wrong when breeding but I needed to add a section about this to help dissuade you from doing this in future.

There is a very old train of thought that suggests every dog should have a litter in its lifetime as this is what is natural. I cannot stress just how much this is the wrong way of thinking. Another factor to this is often I hear from families choosing to breed because they have children and it teaches them about nature and also about responsibilities and it's nice to have the puppies around. My argument here is you are merely teaching them how to be irresponsible in breeding and just how easy it is to do.

I will hold my hands up and say I have not always been the best of breeders and I still could do better! However, I'm sure you know I know more than most and I have sadly lost my bitch through the birthing process in the past, something I would not wish upon anyone and while this happens to even the best of breeders it's a horrific thing to experience. Do you want to subject your children or in fact yourself to that grief when it could be avoided?

There are already way too many puppies out there that will unfortunately spend their lives in less than adequate care and less than perfect health due to less than perfect breeding practices - these puppies are the most likely to either be put to sleep or end up in rescue.

To be an amazing breeder requires years of study and thousands of pounds and hours of effort, sweat and tears.

You now also need a licence to breed from your local council which is very expensive and time consuming.

The basics are getting the health tests done and picking the right mate for your dog and considering temperament and vetting homes for puppies. This takes time and money. And seriously that's not even 20% of the things you need to do and know to get it right.

Male dogs

I have Moss, my very own stud dog and there is one litter I should have never let him sire, I did and I regret it to this day. I also know many puppies have been bred from these puppies and not in a good way either - that weighs very heavy indeed, each day of my life. I hate that I did that, when I could have chosen not to. I did know better. Once you have used your dog at stud you can expect behaviour changes, for their testosterone will be at peak levels for at least four months after. What's more is that they will have 'had a test for it' and be very distracted whenever a bitch is in season in the area. Not great when you just want to enjoy long walks with your pet dog.

Female dogs

Not only do you risk losing your bitch through birth but you risk losing some or all of the puppies, you could end up hand rearing them, you could need to pay for a caesarean. You could end up paying for a caesarean, hand rearing puppies and still lose both the bitch and the puppies - it happens and more than you would think!

Even when things go well, I have seen bitches visibly age after a litter. Despite only being three years of age but acting and looking like a ten-year-old dog - do you really want that for your beloved pet?

By breeding from your pet, you are bringing new life into the world and that's a lot of responsibility. Do you have the knowledge and experience to support puppy owners throughout their lifetimes? Do you have the space and funding to be able to accommodate puppies being returned due to a change in circumstances, even 5 or 8 years later? This could be two or three in each litter!

Conversely these are all things that you need to be thinking about when you meet a breeder - are they knowledgeable, are the supportive and do they offer to take the puppy back if at any point you are unable to keep them anymore?

Breeding endorsements on KC registered puppies

This can be a confusing subject, but I wanted to help you to understand.

When a breeder registers a litter with the Kennel Club they can tick a box to prevent you from registering any puppies you may breed from your puppy in future.

These restrictions/endorsements can be removed at the discretion of the breeder in future, and the breeder should include a discussion about this with you when you purchase the puppy whether verbally or as part of the sales contract.

Placing endorsements or restrictions on puppies is a responsible thing to do. It discourages buyers purchasing a puppy to breed from irresponsibly in the future. It also helps to safeguard the breed line that the breeder may have spent decades developing and protecting.

There is another side to this, which now you know what it means will help to explain why you will see many litters advertised for sale where the 'breeder/greeder' has paperwork for both parents, they are both registered with the Kennel Club but the puppies are not. They are not eligible for registration due to endorsements on the paperwork. I encourage you to avoid these kind of breeders as they will not have the best interests of the puppies at heart – only their bank balance unfortunately.

Puppy Prepared?

9 AVOID THESE COMMON PITFALLS

Stress on the bitch during pregnancy

A bitch who has been under stress during her pregnancy will produce pups that are not as resilient to stress and who are more likely to not only suffer with immune related health issues but also suffer with behaviour issues too. These puppies are often highly strung and struggle to relax or switch off when required or needed.

It's worth keeping this in mind if you go for a puppy that has been born into rescue. The mother has likely been under stress when stray or when handed in and then had to adjust to a kennel environment.

Stress is part of everyday life for humans and for dogs but in small quantities, undue stress on a bitch would affect puppies and their development. The bitch being ill during pregnancy. More examples of stress on a bitch during pregnancy are as follows - a house move, the loss of another dog in the household, owner going on holiday/change of routine. As much as possible the bitch should be keep to her normal routine with meals being increased in the later stages of pregnancy, with reducing amounts of exercise.

Fern's Story

After we lost Jazz during childbirth in 2011 (giving us Moss and his four brothers) I was on the lookout for another bitch to possibly show and to breed from in future. The plan was to breed her to Moss so I could carry on my line.

I became friends with a lady who showed mini long Dachs and was a professional dog groomer. I helped her out a couple of times when she had staff off on holiday in the grooming salon and although I was already grooming professionally, I can always learn more so shadowed her too. She was kind enough to let me stay at her house in these times as it was around a 3-hour drive from home. I got to know her Dachs pretty well and also stayed with her for support a couple of times when her bitches were due to whelp/have puppies.

One of the bitches she had was called Grace and she was a beautiful black and tan girl. She would be glued to the breeder's side whenever she was sat on the sofa or clinging to her heels in general. Always longing to be by her owner.

Grace was born as a singleton puppy. Singleton puppies come with issues! They have not had other puppies to interact with in the whelping box, they have not learnt how to play properly, nor learnt that life isn't fair sometimes by being pushed off the milk bar etc. Most singleton pups suffer greatly when faced with frustration. This can make them vocal and sometimes sharp/aggressive if work hasn't been put in early.

Grace was a lovely dog but had faults – mainly due to her being an only pup. After a whole week of staying with the breeder and all of the dogs (who would join us everywhere we went) if I just left the room for a moment, go to the toilet for example and then reappear Grace would spend a whole 20 minutes barking at me, no matter what the breeder did to try and stop her, she simply would not stop. Twenty whole minutes of barking is not only excessive and not needed but also a very long period of time.

Grace trained me well that week to cross my legs and not leave the room unless I absolutely had to!

Despite all of this, I still put my name down for a puppy from Grace! Yes, really.

I knew what I was signing up for and I still did it – stupidly. Now don't get me wrong, I love the bones off Fern, but she has not been easy, and she will never be an easy dog.

Did I know I was signing up for?

I knew I was signing up for another Grace, another dog who would bark at people coming through doorways.

Why did I still do it?

Because I was cocky. That's the simplest most honest answer I can give.

I was at a stage in my professional development as a trainer that I was overconfident and thought I knew everything.

My peers all said that if a 'behaviour has been imprinted by the mother, you will never train the puppy to not perform that behaviour' my mindset at the time was that they were wrong... Watch me! Not only watch me but I will prove you wrong, and I will 'fix Fern' so much that she I will be able to breed from her with no worries or concerns about the puppies behaviours.

Oh, how wrong I was!

The tears, the frustration, the sheer disappointment that I felt in that first couple of years with Fern. She was the cutest, most attentive little pup, she loved attention and loved everyone but immediately bonded with both me and my hubby Mark. She was an angel...an angel until she hit 14 weeks of age... when she barked at another dog for the first time and then she started to bark at people out and about, then barking at my stepsons (who both lived with us at the time) when they walked through the kitchen door...having only left moments before. Sound familiar? Yep! The perfect little bundle of fur had turned into the nightmare.

Even at this point although disheartened I was still determined – after all despite her not starting these behaviours when she first came home (lulling me into a false sense of security), it is nothing that I didn't expect really.

Imagine that! A trainer with a barky, apparently aggressive puppy?!

The judgements, the comments and the looks that were thrown in our direction. All of which was far from helpful as I'm sure you can imagine. All of her littermates have been re-homed at least once since leaving the breeder and all because of their behaviour.

I spent weeks, months and years working with Fern to improve her behaviour and while yes she is certainly more manageable now – she is far from perfect. We have competed at Crufts together, she was the first Dach bitch of all 6 varieties to achieve her level 6 Rally title and she's done lots of other activities too, so she's not hopeless!

Do we still have the issues of when people walk through the kitchen door? Yes, we do. Is it 20minutes? Thank Dog (see what I did there?) it is not, maybe 30 seconds that is all. She's very loyal, playful and loving girl who is her Daddies little princess. I admit defeat though - they were right, I was wrong – you cannot train them not to do what has been imprinted.

What the hell am I talking about? What is imprinting?

In this example it is one of the first behaviours the pups learn from their mother.

In the pup's eyes they must perform this behaviour in this circumstance because that will keep them safe. Puppy see puppy do – because mum did.

I cannot stress how important this is. What can you learn from me and Fern? Get to know the mother of the puppies, do you like her temperament and her behaviour, if not then don't buy the puppy.

Yes, genetics from both mother and father influence your pup's behaviour and of course the way they are reared with both the breeder and then you will also have an influence, but the bitch's behaviour will always have the biggest influence over anything else. Remember that your puppy may not start to show these behaviours until after you have brought them home, they will usually start to perform these behaviours between 12 and 16 weeks of age - by which point you have had them home for a few weeks and you have bonded with them.

Knowing now what you do about the bitch's stress levels and behaviour it may not be worth you going down the rescue puppy route. There are always homes waiting for puppies from rescue so please don't feel like you have to take it because you feel sorry for it, they will get a good home. If, however you still feel you can and are willing to take on a puppy from rescue then don't let me stand in your way. I hope by reading this book you can then understand what potential issues you may be taking on and how to move forward with its training (more of this in the next book).

Don't get siblings or two pups at once

It's a common thing I see asked on various Facebook groups and that I get asked by friends, acquaintances when they know I'm a dog trainer.

"Should we get two pups so they can keep each other company?" "Is it cruel to take just one away from the litter and mother?" "Surely its nicer for puppy to have a playmate while I'm at work?"

No, Hell No!

Any breeder worth their salt will never sell you two puppies. If they agree to sell you two, maybe even offer you a 'deal' then run for the hills – they are simply breeding for profit and no thought of the pup's welfare, or yours for that matter.

What happens when you get two from the same litter? You are opening yourself up to heartbreak, failure and a lot of hard work. One puppy is hard work, I've never said having a puppy was easy. Having two isn't twice the work but thrice. Not only are you trying to train each dog, but you are then fighting against their desire for them to be together, to play together, be distracted by each other and to get into trouble together.

Think about it this way, they were born together, have been together since that first minute in our world and will rely on each other as a crutch, a source of confidence. They have had 8 – 12 weeks together with their siblings and mother and then embark on a new life with you, the only thing that is familiar is the other pup. This means they are less likely to bond to you for they have the bond with each other. The vision of them keeping each other occupied and entertained when you cannot be there is correct but them hurtling around growling and jumping in play together in front of the tv when you want to relax when you get home, isn't exactly the tired relaxed cute sleeping puppy picture you envisaged, is it?

Play fighting is normal and part of a pup's development while with the litter, but it is not to be encouraged once they are in new homes. It serves an important purpose while with the breeder – to teach boundaries, bite inhibition, dealing with frustration and self-control. Continuing this after is merely learning how to fight your opponent effectively. Harsh maybe, but true. Once hormones start to surface at around 16 weeks of age this play fighting can start to turn more sinister, especially if you have pups of the same sex.

Most common outcomes of having sibling pups –
Aggression/reactivity toward other dogs
Less control / harder to train
Little to no interest in you or other humans
Fights between the two dogs as they get older
They suffer separation anxiety when they do have yo be split up for occasions such as emergency vet visits etc.

Two bitches –
Fights, particularly around seasons. If both spayed still fights often ensue.

Two dogs –
Fights, more so if around a bitch who has not been spayed.

Bitch and a dog –
Less common to have fights but more likelihood of producing inbred and unhealthy puppies if not neutered young (neutering young isn't advisable for their wellbeing either). Separation anxiety while being separated for seasons if not carefully managed early on.

Conversely, I do know people who have had siblings and made it work, however these people are never first-time puppy owners. They are more likely to have done it, made it work through lots of separate training, walks, keeping them separate for large chunks of time while they are young and given the choice would not choose litter-mates again due to the work load that it comes with to get it right.
I could go on and on about this subject and to a certain extent if you are still keep on doing this I strongly suggest you read 'Another Pup?' first to get an idea of the reality and how it can still go wrong of you have chosen the wrong mix of siblings.

It comes back to if you don't have time for one puppy then you certainly do not have time for two.

Feel free to google littermate syndrome if you still need convincing otherwise.

So, if not siblings should you get two pups around the same age?
No.

Although you may have those initial weeks in your favour don't forget that dogs speak dog, they will prefer communicating with each other over looking to you for companionship and guidance. After all, why do you want a dog? To be your best buddy, to be your faithful furry friend? Yep not the other dog's buddy and with you on the outskirts of their world.

Don't buy an only puppy

Hopefully by me sharing Fern's story, and how her mother Grace was an only puppy has started to get the point across about avoiding a puppy that was born as a singleton, no other puppies in the litter, or who survived past the first few weeks.

It is truly amazing how much can influence how your puppy will turn out before you even get them. It's the whole point of this book really, to make you aware that they are not clean slates and if you know what to look for you can make the best decision for you and your household hopefully setting you up for success.

An only puppy has missed out on so much, they have had the milk bar/mum all to themselves, they have not been pushed off the teat and had to scramble back or learn how to be patient, this then causes them to struggle to deal with any amount of frustration when older. This can manifest as throwing a paddy when restrained, for grooming, towelling, being fussed, being on lead and prevented getting to something that they want, for being behind a door or barrier. A pup that isn't able to cope with frustration can be a big problem and they can then turn this frustration into aggression, barking, growling etc.

I am by no means saying they are all like this or to this extent, merely sharing what happens in the worst cases and if not recognised and worked on when they are very young then how it leads to a lifetime of stress and misery for both dog and owner.

Why put yourself through it? I wouldn't and I have the tools and knowledge to help a dog in the situation, but I would never decide on that being the puppy for me no matter how every other box maybe ticked this would be a firm no from me.

Hand reared pups

Hand reared pups also often find it hard to cope with frustration and suffer many of the same issues as singleton pups. While they often had their littermates to play with, the act of humans feeding the pups individually can have negative effects too. I have hand reared my own litter. We unfortunately lost our beloved Jazz during childbirth and she left us with five amazing boys to care for. I was aware of the issues that can be caused by this and I selfishly could not send them to a foster bitch to care for them, at the time they were all I had left of my beautiful girl. From a behaviour perspective and health perspective them going to a foster bitch would have been the better option.

I bottle fed what became known as 'Jazz's gifts' or the 'miracle litter' (a miracle that they all survived) but would let them suckle for a few seconds then remove the bottle, causing them to get a little frustrated at the food/milk being removed before letting them feed again, I would do this numerous times in each feeding session. Now I'm not trying to bash breeders who have not done this in the slightest. Many breeders are not aware and even if they are its totally all-encompassing and exhausting caring for new-born pups. It's 24/7 care for weeks for once you have finished feeding them you are having to try to encourage them to go to the toilet (as the bitch would), because they cannot do this of their own accord under 3 weeks of age. Once this cycle has finished you are often sterilising equipment ready for the next feed and starting over again so adding more complications into this is a huge ask.

I placed lots of little challenges in the pup's way once they were up on their feet and mobile, things they would have to navigate over or around in order to get their food – again to help them deal with frustration.

I have a friend who breeds and rears pups for the police (he's a police dog trainer) and despite their extensive knowledge on this they have yet to hand rear a pup that by the age of 8 months has not had to be euthanised due to aggression and frustration issues. Yes of course they are breeding German Shepherd's and similar breeds, and I bred a litter of little Dachshunds... not the same by any means but my point is just because I managed to with our five and they turned out ok, that's not to say others can or in fact I could again with another litter or another breed. So again, keep it simple – hand reared, no mother – don't buy the pup it's not worth the risk.

10 HOW TO FIND A BREEDER? WHERE TO START!

Commercial versus hobby breeder & the new licensing laws

What is a commercial breeder?

A commercial breeder can come in many forms, from a very unscrupulous puppy farmer to someone who has more than three litters per year. Of either one or more breeds.

What is a hobby breeder?

I am a hobby breeder; my last litter was in 2011 and I plan to breed again in summer 2020. I have a stud dog, Moss who was last used in 2017, just owning a stud dog makes me a breeder - for I help to produce puppies in one form or another.

A hobby breeder maybe someone who simply wants to breed from their pet dog, having never had a litter before. Other hobby breeders maybe someone who has a litter every year simply because they enjoy breeding and having puppies around.

There are also breeders that sit between the two categories.

The recent licensing laws that came into effect in October of 2018 have meant that anyone making more than £1000 profit per year from the sale of puppies has meant that they have a need to be licensed by their local council and while the laws needed to be tightened this has created a double edged sword as some of the very best responsible breeders have now given up breeding. Previously they would only breed every few years when they themselves want a puppy to keep for the next generation and depending on their local council the price to gain a licence is simply too high.

Certain websites / types of advertising for puppies - what to look for & what to avoid

There are many websites out there that advertise hundreds if not thousands of litters for sale online. I'm ashamed to say even I have used them to advertise pups on them in the past. Many of these websites are now flooded with unscrupulous breeders, puppy farmers and people illegally importing puppies from abroad.

While I'm sure some of the website owners do their best to avoid illegal and unscrupulous puppy sellers it's very hard for them to monitor this.

The main sites I encourage you to avoid are as follows - you will notice I am purposely not giving you the full link to them on purpose!

Epupz
Preloved
Pets4Homes
Gumtree

There are too many to list, but these are the most popular and most used sites.

Avoid the following forms of advertising -

- Signs by the side of the road
- Adverts in the paper
- Adverts in local shops

The Facebook rules have also recently changed to not allow adverts or selling of animals through it, including through posts on groups (not just in Facebook Market place) and I would avoid any such listing on social media that may have slipped through the net also.

Best places to look for a responsible breeder

The very best of breeders hardly if ever need to advertise, for they have waiting lists and homes for puppies before they are born. You will find these breeders through breed clubs, attending events and getting to know them personally.

If you are looking for a pedigree puppy -

- The Kennel Club find a puppy service online (link at the back of the book) - though this comes with the temptation to take one of the pups available at the time it is worth visiting or contacting the breeder to discuss plans for a future litter and also 'sounding them out' more to follow on the best way to do this.
- Contacting the breed club, many breed club websites will have a list of breeders and a puppy listing page. Call the breed club puppy secretary to discuss your wants and needs and they should be able to advice you on where to look and who to contact to discuss further.
- Champdogs (again link at the back of the book) - this is a site mainly used by people who breed to better their breed, who are proud of their pedigrees who show or compete with their dogs. You can search for breeders and puppies on this website. You can also see pedigrees of dogs and planned litters too.
- Attend a breed show or event and talk to breeders there.

Talk to owners and ask for recommendations of breeders etc.

If you are looking for a crossbreed –

Most popular crosses will have their own club, a registry of respectable and passionate breeders. Contact their club and chat to them further. Most popular crosses will have annual events or meet ups, go along ask questions ask for recommendations get to know some breeders and owners of these dogs.

'Dog Lovers Registration' - AVOID

This company or organisation is one of a few which enables unscrupulous breeders to claim and advertise their puppies as 'registered pedigrees' giving the impression that they are registered with the Kennel club when they are not. The difference between dog lovers reg (or similar) and KC registered puppies are miles apart. Anyone can register their dog with these organisations and tell them a load of made up dogs that do not exist are in their parentage or pedigree. This is no guarantee of who or what your dog has descended from. There is no checking system, only that the money has been paid for this registration - giving you no peace of mind just a piece of paper that isn't worth anything. Avoid like the plague!

Rare colours & Coat patterns

In many breeds there are rare colours or coat patterns, which can seem very attractive. Some of these will be perfectly fine, others absolutely not. If a breeder is advertising and stating that they have a 'rare puppy' for sale then this is not the type of breeder you are looking for, please avoid. They are breeding purely for money.

In my own breed Dachshunds, there has been a rise in popularity for 'blue' Dachshunds and due to the nature of how closely inbred they are they often suffer skin and health issues which last for the dog's lifetime. Please do not line the pockets of these kind of breeders - or greeders as I like to call them. Similarly, please be mindful of the 'merle' gene (or dapple if we are talking Dachs) this is a beautiful pattern to look at, the most common breed you are likely to see with this is in sheepdogs however two merle/dapple dogs should never be mated together as this will cause puppies with health problems, blindness and deafness being the most common issues but I have also see ones be born malformed physically too. Some breeders will purposely breed in this way as all of the puppies born will be dapple/merle so they can make more money. The KC does not allow the registration of puppies born from such a mating. Puppies from this kind of mating often have more white in their coat than you would normally expect to see in a normal merle coat.

There are also other breeds which have recently been seen with merle coat patterns which have not been in the breed before. This suggests that an outcross has happened at some point (with another breed that has the merle gene). The Kennel club will only allow certain colours and patterns to be registered in the UK for each breed so again please check what the breed standard says. Some puppies can be registered with the KC but will be categorised as 'colour not recognised'. I'm trying hard not to confuse you here as this can get quite complex but essentially if you want a colour or coat pattern that is not common for that breed, look into it and consider what the COI % maybe, how much in breeding has occurred for this to happen and what potential health issues are there because of this?

Puppy Prepared?

11 HOW TO CHOOSE THE BREEDER, WHAT TO LOOK FOR & WHAT TO ASK THEM

Where they are reared matters!

If you live on a farm, then buy a puppy from a farm. If you have kids, a loud busy semi-detached, in a city type of household then buy from the same!

A puppy bought from a farm should be used to the sound of gunshot, heavy farm machinery, wildlife, early starts etc.

A puppy bought from a busy household, people coming and going, music on loud, hearing the traffic outside etc will be used to all of that. The crazy chaotic lifestyle that comes with having young children the noises etc.

If your dog is going to live in a kennel, then buy one that is raised in one. Do not buy one that's raised in a kennel and expect it to settle in a home - it has missed out on so much! We forget just how many strange noises sights and smells that a kennel raised puppy will not have been exposed to when it's brought into the home. Simple things such as taps running, flushing the toilet, the TV, the kettle, dishwasher, washing machine and hoover all of which are every day household items can be perceived as a monster coming to attack them to a pup that has been raised in a kennel, shed, barn or outbuilding.

If you live next to an airfield or a train line this needs to be considered too and while just one or two new things for the pup to deal with is normally ok, if you are buying a pup that is timid and hasn't heard lots of strange noises or seen lots of things in the sky this is very likely going to become an issue.

We live right next to the train tracks. I have never had an issue with pups getting used to this in the ten years have been living here but I got everything else right and each new puppy has had my other dogs to watch and realise they are not bothered which of course has helped (one of the few positives to having multiple dogs as they rarely pick up on the good things from each other - more often the bad habits unfortunately).

DO; (Best practice when finding a breeder).

Ask to see the puppy's mother, which should be present. This is VERY important. The temperament of the puppy mainly comes from the mother. If you don't like the mother's personality, don't buy a pup.

Make sure you view the mother with the pups and that the bitch is in fact the mother. Some very unscrupulous breeders will use an alternative bitch for viewings that may be better looking to try and sell you a puppy. The real mother may not in fact be the breed you are looking for.

See the puppy in the environment it was bred in; the best setting is the FAMILY HOME. If you suspect that the conditions are not right, DO NOT BUY THE PUPPY.

Be prepared to be put on the breeder's waiting list- a healthy puppy is worth waiting for.

Ask if you can return the puppy if things don't work out; a responsible and reputable breeder will always say yes.

Be suspicious of a breeder selling more than one (maximum two) breeds, unless you are sure of their credentials.

Try to go to a Kennel Club Assured breeder or at least a breeder who register their pups with the Kennel Club if you are buying a pedigree dog - while this is no guarantee of a healthy animal, nor any guarantee that they are not a puppy farmer it does weed out the majority.

Ask if the pups and parents have had any relevant health tests AND ASK TO SEE THE RESULTS.

Ask the breeder as many questions as you can. If they are a responsible breeder, they will be pleased to answer them.

Write down any questions you have before you visit the breeder. It's likely that you will forget them while you are there.

Why did they choose to breed their bitch in the first place?

Ask what the breeding was designed to achieve, why the stud was selected for example.

A litter should be bred for a reason. Not only to produce puppies for sale.

What activities do they do with their dogs? Most reputable breeders will compete in some way with their dogs, whether that is showing them or working them.

If possible, ask for contact with a previous buyer from the breeder in order to see a pup from a previous litter.

Ask what socialisation has been done, eg. car rides, meeting people, busy places, vehicles, noises. A new owner should expect a pup to be able to slot into modern life.

What back up does the breeder provide? If there are problems, is the breeder willing to help either by phone or by visits?

Does the breeder want to stay in touch with you and the pup? If not then why not?

Do they provide advice regarding feeding? Will the new puppy come with some food and instructions about nutrition?

Will I get a certificate showing the worming dates for my puppy?

If I take my pup to my vet for a health check and my vet finds something wrong do I get a full refund on the puppy?

Will the dog come with four weeks insurance?

Will my puppy be microchipped? It is now a legal requirement that the breeder needs to microchip puppies before leaving.

Be prepared to answer lots of questions from the breeder! They should be interviewing YOUR suitability to have one of their pups! Do you feel like they are interrogating you? If you do, this is an excellent sign.

Take an experienced behaviourist or a good breeder with you. They won't be emotionally involved and will be able to give you good advice.

DON'T!

Don't buy a puppy from a pet shop – they have often come from puppy farms.

Don't pick your puppy up from a 'neutral location' such as a motorway service station. This is a common tactic used by puppy farmers.

Don't buy a puppy because it is in terrible conditions and you feel sorry for it. It is hard to walk away, but if you buy the puppy, you are perpetuating the problem (and making space for another poor puppy). Leave and report the breeder.

Don't be fooled by a Kennel Club certificate; they are often faked by puppy farmers who are operating illegally and have no qualms about falsifying paperwork. The majority of puppy farmers will not register their litters with the Kennel Club. If in doubt check with the Kennel Club.

www.mykc.org.uk is a wonderful tool to use to check pedigrees, to check if your pup has been registered and of any health tests of the parents. You only need to ask for the bitch/mother of pup's registered name (as long as she is registered with the UK Kennel Club) for you to check more details through this website.

Don't be persuaded by the breeder to have two puppies from the same litter or different litters. It is NOT better to have two puppies together.

Don't buy a puppy with any obvious health issue.

Don't buy a puppy over ten weeks of age. The cut-off point for socialisation is 12-16 weeks.

What to look for in a breeder/puppy when looking for a companion dog

Puppies should be reared in the house – not in a garage/kennel/shed, etc.

Never take home an only pup (only one survived, only one born) unless you are very experienced, if you do, expect to have frustration issues to deal with.

Ideal litter size is 5 for a well-rounded/ temperament puppy (but not a crucial point)

The mother of the pups shows no signs of illness, distress or spooking

The mother should be seen with the pups (not in a separate room to the puppies).

The breeder should have carried out relevant health checks for the breed on both father and mother – this includes health checks for both parents of designer or mixed breeds, etc.

The breeder should ask you about your lifestyle, work hours, intentions for the pup, etc.

The breeder should be able to tell you all about the breed but also should be asking you how much you know about the breed.

Never take the last pup if you have only seen that puppy and not seen it with its littermates.

Try and view the pups before they are old enough to go to new homes, giving you a chance to avoid the temptation of those puppy eyes pleading you to take them home the same day despite many things that may not tick boxes above and below.

It is crucial to have plenty of toys in with the litter at all times.

It is also important that at feeding times there are plenty more bowls than puppies (to reduce the chances of food aggression/guarding when they are older).

The puppies should have two separate surfaces in their pen/area this helps with toilet training to distinguish between places to toilet and sleep

The breeder should offer advice for the lifetime of the dog.

The breeder should not have more than two separate breeds.

If the breeder is breeding more than three litters per year, they should have a licence for some councils.

A breeder ideally should breed no more than two litters per year if that.

Pups should be weaned onto a wide range of different foods to avoid allergies, and puppies should never be weaned onto just one complete diet.

The mother of the puppies can separate herself from the puppies as and when she pleases (even if it is a shelf above the puppies) – not just kept away from them from weaning age, she should still be around the pups to discipline them, etc. up until the time they are ready to leave.

The breeder should be able to tell you of all the places they have taken the pups, i.e., in the car, the vets, the garden and also how many different types of people the puppies have met, young, old, with hats, without, glasses, sticks, different races of people, etc.

The breeder who only offers you a pup on breeding terms should also be avoided. Breeding terms would be something like asking to have the bitch or dog back in future to breed from, or that you breed from them and once they have a puppy back from you they will register your pup (now an adult dog) in your name, the registration stays with the breeder until this time. Often these arrangements involve a lower initial purchase price which can be tempting but they rarely work well in practice.

The breeder can tell you about the different personalities of the pups and advise on which may suit you best.

Expect an ongoing relationship with the breeder - if you don't like them as a person don't bother buying a puppy

Any breeder worth their salt will be keen to stay in contact with you, receive regular updates about the puppy the lovingly brought into the world and be on hand to support and advise you if you get stuck. They should be on hand at every turn and stumbling block, offering knowledge and advice. It's a relationship that should be nurtured, between you and the breeder. If you do not like them, do not agree with their ethics or their practices then there is little point buying a puppy from them as you will be tied to a certain extent to them for the lifetime of your puppy. Yes, in law the puppy is yours once you have handed over the money and taken the puppy home but having the right breeder behind you is worth its weight in gold.

A good breeder will ask you to sign a contract and while, if I'm truly honest very few are actually enforceable, they are a sign of a responsible breeder. Ideally if the contract states something along the lines of if you should ever need to give up your puppy that the breeder should have the first refusal in having the puppy back - this is a very good sign indeed. If the breeder does not discuss this with you or provide you with a contract which includes this, I would be very wary. This shows their commitment to the puppy and to support you. They are showing that they acknowledge the responsibility for bringing life into the world and want to ensure it is cared for throughout its lifetime

Puppy culture

In an ideal world, in my opinion everyone who breed a litter should be doing something like 'the puppy culture protocol' this was something that has been Jane Killion's brainchild. She's an American breeder of English Bull Terriers and is a highly knowledgeable trainer. From the day the puppies are born she is performing exercises with them, right through to when they leave for their new homes. There is a DVD boxset available to buy which takes you through every step of how to put her protocol into practice, and a support group on Facebook for breeders too. She teaches the puppies so many skills which really sets them up for success with their new owners and for life.

Puppy culture helps minimise so many common issues which cause frustration to the new owners and reduces the risk of puppies being re-homed greatly. Puppies are sent home with problem solving skills, patience, how to walk on a loose lead, house trained and crate trained and so much more. However, as this has only been developed and marketed in recent years and primarily in America there are very few breeders in the UK who are aware of it never mind use the program.

There are other similar programs being marketed in the UK that are helpful and useful too, but again that are in diar need of more breeders to partake in these programs. These programs are quite work intensive for the breeder and if you are lucky enough to find such a breeder (they are very few and far between), expect to pay a higher price for a puppy. Remember you are saving yourself lots of time energy and frustration as your puppy will be set up right for life with you.

ENS / Early Neurological Stimulation

This is something that was originally used for American military dogs and consists for spending about 30 seconds doing specific things with each puppy in the first couple of weeks after they are born, doing these exercises once each day. This stimulates parts of their brains which makes dogs more intelligent, easier to train, able to problem solve better and helps build strong immunity too. This is something I do with my own litters and I asked Ripple's breeder to do when she was born, to which she happily obliged. It's so easy and quick to do which such a massive positive effect for puppies and owners - we just need more breeders to do it!

I have provided the link to this study in the back of the book if you want to know more about this, if you meet the breeder before pups are born it would be worth asking them to do this with the puppies if they are not already aware of it.

12 TIMING & WAITING

Waiting versus not

Most people go from deciding they want a puppy to getting one within a month assuming the finances are in place to purchase. With little thought to the lifetime costs of the puppy or the breed, the breeder, age, sex etc., and while some work out fine most don't when you choose a puppy in this manner. Hell, I've been there and done this too! Remember what I told you about how we got Rosco at the start? We wanted a smooth haired but got a longhaired because we were impatient, and it turned out to be from a puppy farm?

The research is key! Which in turn makes you wait. Even researching isn't always a guarantee. When I had Bella euthanised, I was devastated but I also knew that I could not imagine lifelong term without a big dog around. I knew I wanted something that would be sociable with everyone and everything (which Bella wasn't in the end) and something that could come out with me on lots of walks each day as I was on 4-5 daily dogs walks as part of my business at the time. In reality, I didn't want a puppy, but circumstances dictated otherwise so I decided on a puppy.

Next was to decide what breed. I knew I wanted a breed and not another crossbreed, not that cross breeds are bad, Bella was such but

I didn't want anything like Bella to avoid me comparing the two, this also helped me decide the sex of what I wanted, I wanted something different so opted for a dog/male.

I researched breeds and knew a lot about breed traits at this point. My dream dog at the time was a big black fluffy bear of a Newfoundland but I also knew that my tiny end terrace in Manchester wasn't going to accommodate one and had no visions of moving in the near future. Although all the traits and temperament of a Labrador was what I was looking for I decided against one as I didn't want something normal, something that you see every day. I love, absolutely adore Labs, but such was my mentality at the time that I didn't want something that every other person had, and if I'm totally honest I'm still the same! That's just me. A Springer wasn't my choice and never would have been but Mica came with the package of being with Mark, I love the bones off her, she is amazing and a true individual, not a 'normal Springer' but I would have never chosen one as there are so many around. Back to the point. I didn't want a Lab, but I wanted the easy going, accepting temperament along with the stamina. This led me to looking at other Retrievers. Labs are Retrievers but it's not common knowledge that there are also 5 other types of retrievers, not just the Golden Retriever and the Lab. There are Curlycoat retrievers (which I love and have very almost had one since), Chesapeake Bay Retrievers, Nova Scotia Duck Tolling Retrievers and Flatcoat Retrievers. I looked again at all of them and narrowed down to either a Duck Toller or a Flatcoat (Flatty), Tollers being slightly smaller and generally a red colour, for me this was similar to Bella despite the difference in coat length. Flatties being for the most part black with the occasional liver/chocolate colour.

I grew up with a black Lab cross called Sheba, and my Dad had a black long coat German Shepherd for a while so I had and always will have a soft spot for black dogs, long coated being my preference, this compounded with some experience of some bouncy young Flatcoats that I cared for when I worked in kennels and the fact that the breed was partly made up from Newfoundlands originally, it made sense to decide on a Flatty. I proceeded to go on a website called Epupz, I had found Jazz through this previously so thought I would be a good place to start.

I emailed every Flatty breeder listed with the same template email, explaining my wish for a puppy, a black male, what dogs I had at the time, my profession and what kind of home I could provide. I wanted to meet the bitch before puppies arrived as I had done some homework and wasn't in an immediate rush as I wanted to get it right. I received a handful of responses from breeders who were not planning to breed in the next 12 months some who were but one stood out, someone who also bred miniature long haired dachshunds as well (as you know, I had two of these at the time – Jazz and Ziggy) and had just mated their liver bitch and were expecting mainly black puppies in a few weeks. She invited me to come and meet the bitch. She ticked the boxes which I had in my mind. She was about an hour and a half away but that was doable. My thinking was if she also has mini long Dachs not only was I getting the breed I wanted but it would be reared with the breed it would be coming to its new home with – my two, so would be even more accepting. I went to meet the breeder and Ruly – the lovely liver bitch. I spent some time there and loved the bitch, I also met the father and was happy. The breeder asked me relevant questions and offered to sell me a signed copy of her good friends' book, which was all about the breed, which of course I happily purchased. The first line of the book went a little like this – if you don't want a clown of a dog, don't get a Flatcoat. A sense of humour and plenty of patience is needed. Oh, how right I would find that line to be! I agreed to put my name down for one of the puppies, the breeder said she would be in touch when the puppies were born, and I went on my way. A few weeks later she told me ten puppies were born and was shocked at the amount of liver puppies – eight! And that there was only one black boy, the remaining black puppy obviously being a girl.

I visited to view the litter when they were just a week old and instantly fell in love with the only black boy, I mean who wouldn't – a tiny black boy puppy. I named him Merlin and visited every week until he was seven weeks when I was allowed to bring him home (this was before the rule was in force that you cannot take a puppy away before 8 weeks).

All went well you are thinking. In many ways yes, he was what I wanted and he eventually grew up to be an absolute legend and gentleman but…there are a few factors here – I was warned by a trainer friend of mine at the time not to get a Flatty as ' they are big, giddy, bouncy and hard work' and he really did test my patience and skill set in his former years. Was that the right breed for me at the time, probably not but he has also shaped me as a trainer so I wouldn't change it. Another part to this was, as he grew and as I became more knowledgeable of the breed and made more contacts within the breed, the more I found that the breeder despite appearances was a high-volume breeder and maybe not the most responsible or ethical. My dealings with the breeder over the years got worse and worse, Christmas cards from them asking if I knew anyone wanting to buy a puppy, they were selling so they could pay the mortgage! In my book if you are breeding pups to make a living you are going to make questionable decisions out of necessity to pay bills.

At the age of three Merlin was diagnosed with a slipped disc and I did the responsible thing and rang the breeder to let her know. I didn't do this in an accusing manner, simply to let her know in case she had experienced similar from any others in the line which you would hope in that case would help her make decisions with regard to future breeding and matings as it isn't a common issue within the breed. Her response? – "do you think you maybe did too much with him when he was young?" In other words, putting the blame back on me, rather than the desired response of ok what a shame, thank you for letting me know or similar. Since I have found other dogs from the same lines with similar issues. Now don't get me wrong I would not change Merlin and our time together for anything, in fact he is the subject of a future book, but if I had spent more time researching the breed and breeders, spent more time with the breed and visited more than one breeder I would have ended up with a healthier dog and a more responsible breeder to purchase from.

Research, research, research!!! I cannot stress this enough.

Winter puppy or Summer puppy?

It makes a difference! There are pros and cons to both. I personally prefer a winter pup but that's just me, it's what works for you and we are all different.

Puppies who go to their new homes in autumn, wintertime are usually a lot better at being handled, towelled off, groomed and bathed. They are more resistant to extreme weather in their confidence and willingness to go out in the rain and wind, and also in the dark. They are also usually more laid back about fireworks, bangs etc. This is because most events that feature fireworks are in the winter and this is before pup has reached their teenage, and potential second fear phase (neural pruning when they are reaching maturity).

The downside for us is those awful long dark evenings. The late-night trips outside freezing while housetraining. A winter puppy owner is also on the back foot with a distinct lack of daylight hours to fit the all-important socialisation in with people, environments, animals, traffic etc.- alongside trying to work and have a life too. Winter pups are also less likely to come across lots of dogs and people on walks and learn how to deal with those situations from a frustration perspective as we simply see less dogs and people out on walks than we would in the summer.

Summer puppies – it's what I like to call puppy season, many people will buy their puppies at this time with the longer days and for some the school holidays around the corner to spend time training and playing with pup. Having longer days and warmer weather for those countless trips to the garden when housetraining is certainly a positive. More dogs and people out on the streets which help with exposing a young pup to all the sights and sounds we want them to accept and behave around. The downside to this is as all the positives I have listed in the winter puppy section you do not have the luxury of. It's hard to remember to make that effort to get them used to being towelled, washed off and groomed more regularly if there is little need with dryer weather over the summer. Puppy reaches the adolescent phase, pushing boundaries, almost rebellious as winter hits and we are asking more of them which is against their nature at that age - to sit/stay still and be messed with. Many are likely to be at the stage of neural pruning (where the brain is maturing and sorting the files it needs and doesn't need, things it needs to fear for survival reasons or not) when bonfire night hits with the fireworks and all the scary Halloween masks at the end of October. This can cause a lifelong fear of such things and events if not managed correctly, just from a case of bad timing.

Neither is right or wrong, it's more a case of considering these things when you are thinking about when to add a puppy to your household and plan accordingly to try and counteract the downsides.

How do you keep yourself occupied when you are waiting?

Do more research, spend time with the breed, go to breed shows or competitions, make friends with breeders and owners. Ask more questions. You can do all of this ensuring you are getting the right pup for you and you can also do what I did, and my good friend Lillie is currently doing… nesting.

I waited just over three years for Ripple to arrive. Three whole years! I had obviously had the breed before and I had spent many hours with the breeder (and others), she had used my boy Moss with her girl Tikka, she had had puppies and she had kept one back for herself - Sophie. Sophie was and still is the spitting image of my Moss and has the same calm confident nature. I had visited the breeder a few times and got to know Sophie more before deciding I wanted a pup out of the same parents - 'let's get me a Sophie' was my thinking, or in a way at least. I think by the time a was certain I wanted a pup from this mating Sophie was 1year old - so the real waiting was for two years and not three. Lisa (the breeder) had already said she wanted to repeat the same mating and I of course shared my intention of having one the next time.

A few things, well life got in the way for a couple of seasons and then Lisa brought Tikka around once again for Moss to do his thang, unfortunately he did not do it and we thing that in fact Tikka was already past that point in her season to accept a mate, so that was another season down the drain and more waiting to do. Seven months later and many visits to ensure we didn't miss the right window, Moss mated her twice and a few weeks later I got confirmation from Lisa that Tikka was pregnant. Still though there was no guarantee of any girls and I only wanted a girl so I know I would have to go on the search again if Tikka did not have a girl this time as it was to be her final litter.

Now you have the back story I'll tell you how I managed to wait that long. Despite all the patience in the world for dogs and training etc, I am not a patient person, it's just not me! I started to nest... because I'm OCD, sad, obsessive whatever you want to call it my dogs are all 'colour coded'. In other words, they all have a colour assigned to them so they have a colour set for their collars, leads, coats, clickers etc. I had decided on pink for the new pup, a bright vibrant pink. We only actually named her Ripple just after she was born, when we knew Fern was to be called that a good few months before she was even made.

Every dog show or event I went to in that two-year period, I was collecting and purchasing pink things. Ripple had four or five collars and leads (for each stage of her growth) four harnesses, three coats, a pink crate, a pink soft crate, a pink hooded bed, over a dozen pink toys, two pink clickers and my friend Deb had even bought me pink Dach socks and a pink Dach T-shirt that were with struct instructions to be saved until she finally became part of the Bartlett zoo. Honestly, I collected two big boxes worth of stuff for Ripple before she was even born. It gave me something to focus on, stopping me from being stupid and just going to buy any Dach puppy I could find.

My good friend, and fellow KCAI Trainer Lillie is waiting for a puppy now out of Ripple, we are very similar - she doesn't do patience and is very excited. We were expecting puppies at the end of this year from Ripple, but she came into season early which means we are now waiting until next year before mating her - more waiting for Lillie. Even before we had to postpone Ripple puppies, Lillie had already decided on teal as the colour for the puppy and is currently nesting. She has already built a good collection of teal things for puppy and I'm sure this will at least double before they arrive next summer. Another bonus to nesting is that you are spreading the initial cost over a greater period of time so when pup does come it's not such a big outgoing. Your bank balance will thank you!

13 SOCIALISATION & VACCINATIONS

Vaccinations, immunity and the risks

Your puppy, provided you have made the right choice and your pup managed to ingest some of the mothers first milk after birth (this first milk is called colostrum and is the way in which the mother passes on immunity to diseases to their pups, to protect them). The mother's immunity will help your puppy for the first few weeks of life, commonly up to around 15-16 weeks of age though this can be a shorter period.

Ziggy, I had vaccinated as a pup and every year until he was 4, when the day after his vaccination he had his first epileptic fit. He has suffered with epilepsy ever since and while we will never know for certain of the vaccination was in fact the cause it was a very close occurrence and I err on the side of caution. He has not been vaccinated since but still shows excellent immunity levels when tested. It's very common for dogs to suffer from over vaccination (also known as Vaccinosis). Particularly smaller dogs. Vaccinations are given in the same doses no matter the size of dog. If we give them medications, then its normally dosed according to their weight. The same dose of vaccine is given to Great Danes as it is to Chihuahuas. The ingredient used to hold the vaccine is mercury. Yes really! Each time our dogs have a vaccination they are being poisoned with mercury and it's this that causes the harm.

There are alternative options to vaccination but again this is your choice and I beg you please do your own research. A great book to read on this subject is 'What vets don't tell you about vaccines' by Catherine O'Driscoll (link at the end of the book) she also has plenty of free resources on her website Canine Health Concern.

Common adverse reactions to vaccinations:
- Lethargy
- Hair loss, hair colour change at injection site
- Fever
- Soreness
- Stiffness
- Refusal to eat
- Conjunctivitis
- Sneezing
- Oral ulcers

Moderate Reactions:
- Immunosuppression
- Behavioural changes
- Vitiligo
- Weight loss (Cachexia)
- Reduced milk production
- Lameness
- Granulomas/Abscesses
- Hives
- Facial edema
- Atopy
- Respiratory disease
- Allergic uveitis (Blue eye)

Severe Reactions triggered by Vaccines:
- Vaccine injection site sarcomas
- Anaphylaxis
- Arthritis, polyarthritis-HOD hypertrophy Osteodystrophy
- Autoimmune Haemolytic Anaemia

- Immune Mediated thrombocytopenia (IMTP)
- Haemolytic Disease of the new-born (Neonatal Isoerythrolysis)
- Thyroiditis
- Glomerulonephritis
- Disease or Enhanced Disease which with the vaccine was designed to prevent
- Myocarditis
- Post vaccinal Encephalitis or polyneuritis
- Seizures
- Abortion, congenital anomalies, embryonic/fetal death, failure to conceive fertility

It is worth me mentioning that there is a test available called a titre test, a blood test to check your dog's immunity levels for these diseases. Testing and then only vaccinating if and when needed is a safer option in my opinion.

Vaccicheck is the cheapest and most widely available so ask your vet about this and get them to order it in if they have not heard of it. This enables them to test in house making the test considerably more cost effective rather than the alternative of sending the bloods to an external lab.

I have Fern who has never been vaccinated in her life, but her Titre tests come back with good results for immunity, so I have no need to vaccinate. She is now six and has been to Crufts, and to countless dog shows and places up and down the country with me.

Moss who did not get the colostrum from his mother due to her passing away during caesarean has had one vaccine for Parvo when he was around 6 months of age. His titre results still come back positive, he has also been everywhere with me, including Crufts for 7 of his 8 years.

Ripple has only ever had one vaccination at 16 weeks of age and now at 2 years old she shows positive immunity when titre tested.

There are two more diseases which are commonly vaccinated for and they are Leptospirosis (Weils disease) and Kennel cough.

Leptospirosis

This is most commonly found in areas with stagnant water and can be contracted from rats. Ask your vet how many cases of this they have seen in your area over the last couple of years and then consider how likely they are to come into contact with it. Will you be walking in areas that are likely to have stagnant water? Or areas with a high population of rats? This is a vaccination that is advised to be administered annually, though there is no proof of it providing immunity for more than a couple of months. A Lepto vaccine called 'Lepto 4' has caused a high rate of serious side effect, including many deaths over recent years. Ask your vet which type they are using.

I have to mention that Lepto is in fact a zoonosis - this means it is one of the few diseases that are contractible to humans too, you can catch this from your dog and vice versa. You must make that decision as to what you feel is the safest. There is no titre test for Lepto.

Kennel Cough

Very similar to the flu jab for humans, it is a live vaccine and only offers immunity for a few strains (there are many strains of kennel cough) so having your dog vaccinated for KC is no guarantee that they will not contract it, just like you can still get the flu despite having the jab. Your dog may show symptoms for the first week or two after it has been administered, though these will be very minor symptoms this also often makes them infectious to other dogs. My experience of it is if your dog have been vaccinated for it and is exposed to it, it may only suffer a milder version of it but still show symptoms and can pass it onto others. This is a highly contagious bug. While it does pose a serious threat to very young dogs and the very elderly, for a fit adult dog it is much like the common cold in us and will pass with restricted exercise and rest. There is no titre test for kennel cough

You can report any suspected adverse side effects from vaccination both to your vet and yourself online for future study via Defra (link in the back of the book).

With all of this in mind, I acknowledge that I am very fortunate that I have care for my dogs when we are away and in case of emergency either with care at home or them going to friends' houses. If I had to place my dogs in kennels, send them to a home boarder or to a day care establishment their licensing dictates that all core vaccines including Lepto and KC/kennel cough must be current and up to date. This is worth considering carefully too, what care will you have in place?

I will never be able to travel abroad with my dogs as I refuse to vaccinate them to the extent that the pet passport scheme dictates. The pet passport scheme allows travel all over Europe with your dog (this is correct at the time of printing but Brexit may change this) and I know many people who either compete, show or holiday with their dogs in France, Spain and further afield so this is important to them. An additional vaccine often needed for overseas travel is the rabies vaccine.

Dogs travelling abroad can be more susceptible to both tick-born and localised diseases.

A note if your breeder has already ensured first vaccines have been administered before your pup comes home

This is common practice amongst most breeders. However, many new pup owners experience problems with this.

The breeder has been responsible by starting vaccinations and passed the vaccination certificate to new owners when they take puppy home with them. Puppy owners then take puppy to the vet for their second set of jabs, only to be met with resistance from the vet. Many vets will use different brands and vaccine protocols, some only advising two vaccinations for a puppy course some up to four according to the manufacturer's instructions. If your vet does not use the same brand as the brand used already on your puppy, then often a new course is the advice from the vet to be started from scratch. This presents a double risk to your puppy. The first risk being over vaccination (increased likelihood of side effects which can sometimes be behaviour issues not just physical health) and the second postponing the time from which your vet deems it safe for you puppy to meet the world and are classed as fully vaccinated. If you come across this situation, I would advise you to call around your local vets to see if they use the same brand as what your puppy has already had. This does not mean you need to use this same vet for the dog's lifetime if you do not want, merely just use them for their puppy vaccinations. Finding a vet that uses the same brand and protocols as what you have already used is the simplest solution to a very common problem.

Socialisation:

In my view and experience there are many more dogs dying (being euthanised) due to not being socialised at a young enough age which in turn causes behaviour issues than there are being put to sleep due to not being vaccinated and have contracted a core disease.

Again, this is your choice, I am not advising either way on this matter. Only asking for you to consider further and I will share my own experiences on it.

Professionally I see far too many puppies who have only come home from the breeders and been to the vets and back a couple of times before 12 weeks of age.

These puppies turn out to have fears and phobias of many things outside of the house because they were not exposed to them often and in a in a positive way under 12 weeks of age. This often causes serious behaviour issues, that last a lifetime.

I do recognise that people with the perfect puppy are less likely to call me, most people who ask for help from a professional are experiencing issues with their puppy or dog. I will always see the negative side more than the positive.

This really saddens me when it could so easily be avoided. Owners will follow the advice from the vet of 'not allowing them out till a week after the puppy course of vaccinations are complete' at best this means puppy is allowed out at 11 weeks and at worst with one courses of vaccinations this can be as late as 15 weeks.

No vet should administer a vaccination to an unhealthy dog. What if your pup contracts a tummy bug and this postpones vaccinations by a week? A week may not seem like a lot, but it truly is when as such an impressionable age.

The optimum socialisation period is from 3-12 weeks, for some breeds, this can go on until 16 weeks. During this time the more, short positive experiences they can have with the big wide world the better. Different types of people, traffic, pushchairs, wheelchairs, horses, other species, weather, sounds, smells the better. The key thing to remember is short periods of exposure, positive (if they are not scared) and with plenty of opportunity to sleep/rest between new experiences. Socialisation to the world is the most important thing and should be prioritised above all else while in this age bracket, they can learn to sit and wait, etc. later. Correct socialisation can be the difference between a lifelong happy, well-rounded companion or an insecure or aggressive shaking wreck. After 12 weeks socialisation should continue, for months if not years but what pup learns in the initial window is the basis for everything else.

If you are bringing puppy home at 8 weeks its worth keeping in mind that you can take them to friends' houses... after all that puppy could have gone to it new home in any of those houses, how is it any different? Carrying your puppy out and about letting it see traffic, people, wheelie bins etc is not putting it at risk of infection, it is in your arms, not on the floor. Taking it for regular short trips in the car is very beneficial also.

Ripple

Ripple went on her first trip to the pub just a day after she came home. She slept through most of it, but she got to meet the staff and other pub goers, she got to see the sights, smell the smells and hear the sounds of that environment. She came with me on her first carriage drive just two days after coming home. She was at her first puppy class (again mainly sleeping) before 10 weeks of age. The list of things we did together in these initial weeks is endless.

I did put her on the floor, despite not being vaccinated. She travelled with me in the van whenever I was out and about and obviously needed to toilet from time to time so she was placed on the floor in areas where I weighed up how likely it was that lots have dogs may have been there or not. Puppies spend a lot of those initial weeks sleeping, and exposure to new things should be positive and brief.

My logic was that her mother had been vaccinated and she had received colostrum and would be covered under her mother's immunity for a minimum of a couple of weeks after she came home. It was my choice to expose her to calculated risks in order to ensure that she tuned into a well-rounded adult dog. She was vaccinated at 16 weeks with just one shot after I had done further research and discussed with my holistic vet.

Personally as harsh as it sounds, I would much rather risk my dog contracting a disease and potentially dying at a young age with the payoff being a well-rounded and confident adult if she didn't contract the disease, than spend the next 15 years with a dog who struggled to cope with life in a human world.

Initial fear period - worth noting!

Puppies will go through a natural stage in their development at around 8 weeks of age. This is one of the reasons why I have brought home my puppies at 7 weeks, though this is not as per current guidelines now.

It's a stage in which they become spooked by things they were previously ok with; this can last for a day or up to a week. Some pups will go through this stage before 8 weeks some after, but the average is 8 weeks. Keep this in mind when they are experiencing what is essentially some very drastic changes, being taken from mother, littermates and its familiar environment. Have patience with them when they settle in at home with you. If you notice them becoming scared maybe just spend a couple of days at home with them before then taking them out to meet the world again, so they don't get more fearful of things. This phase passes very quickly. I took Ripple out to so many places almost straight away because she was such a confident little character, and because I had spent so much time with her while at the breeders, we had bonded, and she had trust in me to keep her safe. I had also provided the breeder with her soft crate to feed her in and allow her to get used to it in small doses before I brought her home. Taking the soft crate with me on the road so she could sleep in it and relax, meaning she felt even more secure as it was so familiar to her.

14 **EXERCISE**

Exercising a puppy shaped jelly

Exercise for your pup - how much is too much? Often less than you think

> ***The very general rule and probably the easiest to remember is 'the 5 minute rule.'***

Only walk your pup for 5 minutes for each month of life. For example, a 6-month-old puppy should only be having 30 minutes exercise (5 minutes x 6 months = 30 minutes). This should be for all breeds up to Labrador size up until 12 months of age, and for larger breeds such as Newfoundlands, Great Danes, St Bernards, etc. up to 2 years of age.

The five-minute rule is great, an even better guide to work from is the Puppy Culture puppy exercise guide which you can buy online or view on google images. It's very specific with types of exercise and size of dog and age of the dog.

> <u>Why? Because puppy's bones and joints are still developing, they are very soft and can easily be damaged.</u>

I have done it all wrong before, as I said at the start - with Ziggy when he was a tiny pup, I took him out with my bigger, older dog Bella every day for an hour, Bella would chase a ball back and forth for the whole of the walk, and Ziggy would chase behind her. I did this from a young age (maybe 4/5 months old) and I remember taking him to the vet for something routine at around 8 or 9 months old and saying to the vet, 'I'm sure I'm over exercising this pup' (I was not working with dogs professionally then, and knew very little, other than I wanted the very best for my dogs and had limited knowledge). The vet responded with something like, 'oh he's a small dog, he will let you know when he's had enough, don't worry about it'. At age 18 months Ziggy was diagnosed with arthritic hips, and this was due to my naivety of over exercising him while he was still growing and maturing.

Ziggy isn't, never has and never will be the type of dog who will let me know when he's 'had enough' he would go all day if I let him, he's still a bouncy, happy chap at 14 years of age but when he does 'overdo it' he is stiff that evening or the next day. The five-minute rule is becoming more and more common knowledge, which is great, but there is still the misconception that it only applies to big dogs. It refers to all sizes, as Ziggy and many others have proven.

Think about it in human terms. You would not ask a 5-year-old child to walk for 10 miles, would you? Nor would you ask a 10-year-old child to carry a heavy load.

Other things to consider while the pup is still growing are things like how often they are jumping off furniture, if you are allowing them to jump in and out of vehicles, playing with other dogs and going up and down stairs. All of these things have an impact on their joints and should be kept to an absolute minimum while young to ensure long-lasting health in their adult life.

During this phase, there is nothing wrong with occasionally meeting up with friends and their adult dogs (provided that they are good role models for the pup of course) and going for a short stroll or meeting at a cafe or pub or going around to their house for a catch-up. This teaches the puppy that other dogs are ok too but putting a lot of importance on not doing this where the other dog is still young and very playful.

In dog agility you are not allowed to compete with your dog until they are 18 months of age, this is due to the wear and tear on their bodies when jumping/landing, twisting and turning through weaves and doing a tight turn to the next piece of equipment. In most other dog sports, there is a minimum age limit to compete and another to move up a level too. Again, due to their bodies maturing, and to help prevent damage.

While some of the above will only apply to when you get puppy home its worth considering some these things now. No matter what breed or size of dog you are hoping to join your family all of the above needs to be considered and planned for in advance. I guarantee you as soon as you mention to your other dog owning friends that you are planning to get a pup they will be at the very least thinking about how you can get your puppy 'localised with theirs' and more than likely suggesting times dates and places you can go and meet up to ensure your puppy is 'socialised properly' because ' it worked for their dog' it may have been ok for their dog but it may not for yours. Set the boundaries now. Blame it on me! 'Sarah said we shouldn't do X because of Y and I plan to stick to it…Sorry!'

Easy clean/Slippy flooring

Ceramic or stone tiles, laminate flooring, linoleum and polished wooden flooring all pose a risk to your pup's health if not managed

Having floors that are slippy are not good for a growing puppy, nor an adult dog.

Although great for cleaning up accidents and maybe cute to watch your pup slide around as they take a corner too fast etc it's not good for their skeletal development nor their confidence. Consider whether you need to by some cheap non slip mats to help your pup get around. I say cheap due to risk of chewing and if pup has an accident on them. Ideally some that are small enough for you to put in the washer from time to time but also heavy enough that your pup does not get into the habit of pulling them around everywhere.

Accidents, strains and injuries are very easy when they are so young and just putting somethings in place to avoid this for something that is easily avoidable is certainly worth thinking about and acting on.

An alternative option would be to regularly put paw wax on your pups paws each day, so they have more grip and you don't have to worry about mats and extra rugs etc.

.

15 CHOOSING THE PUPPY – IDENTIFYING THE INDIVIDUAL WITHIN A LITTER

I would always advise you to go and view the litter between 3 & 5 weeks and again around 6-8 weeks before making a final choice. This means 3 visits in total as a minimum, bringing puppy home on the 3rd visit.

Now, once you have met the mother of the pups and are happy with her temperament and happy with the breeder and set up how do you pick which puppy to take home? They are all cute and mischievous at 6-8 weeks when most people view a litter, so it's hard to know which one is a good fit for them. The choice you make is crucial, just as crucial as the mother, the breed and the breeder selection. Of course, most people have a preference on colour or coat pattern from an aesthetic point of view and also a preference on a boy or a girl, there is nothing wrong with this at all.

If this is your first dog, then the difference between dogs and bitches would be worth considering

Bitches are generally smaller than Dogs. I personally prefer dogs despite only having bitches as a child.

Dogs are more about strength and protection while bitches are more about providing and hunting. This is a very loose and general rule so I would take it with a pinch of salt, or at least keep it in the back of your mind.

In general, male dogs will bond better with female owners and bitches bonding more with men – though again this is negligible. Bitches come with seasons which can be messy in some girls, and while you may be choosing to get them spayed in future, I would advise you to wait at least two seasons before you do this. Male dogs are harder work while they are going through the adolescent phase with high testosterone levels, but this does subside. Frequent stops to mark or tinkle on lampposts and such like on walks can be expected throughout their lifetimes. I find male dogs are easier to housetrain than females.

Bitches can have more slightly manipulative traits while male dogs are more likely to use their strength rather than brains to outwit you if they decide to (again – a reminder that I normally only see the worst behaved dogs due to the nature of my job, not the good ones). Please don't let any of this discourage you from having a dog they are merely minor, and subtle differences I find between the two sexes.

Not many to choose from?

If there are slim pickings within the litter leaving with only one that you like should you just take that one? Not necessarily, you may need to wait until the next litter if you want the best possible puppy for you - after all this is hopefully going to be part of your family for the next 10-15years (breed dependant).

Character selection

Commonly if you are choosing a breed like a Labrador there may be many to choose from. You want a black boy and have 6 black boys to choose from, how do you choose?

As with most things the answer is 'it depends'. Assuming you are picking a suitable breed for you and your lifestyle we now need to look at your personality as much as a puppy's character. It is possible to get a picture of their future character even at such a young age.

I won't go through every character but here are the main ones to look for.

I encourage you to be honest with yourself too. What type of person you are and how your personality may match to each pup. Or not as the case maybe.

Pup 1 -The first puppy to run and greet you - often the one that people claim 'the puppy picked them'. A confident bold character, often quite chunky in build to its littermates, inquisitive, not fazed by much at all. Not for a quiet, sensitive person. Best suited to a strong character of person, who will establish boundaries fairly. Very suited to dog sports or as a working dog. Very intelligent and straight forward to train but the owner must have clear rules and be consistent.

Pup 2 - Rushes out to greet you (often just behind Pup 1) then quickly runs back, slightly nervy, jumpy and nippy. This one is one to avoid for most people, including most trainers. Not an easy dog to own! Constantly testing everyone and everything. Thrives on routine. If you do choose this one its best with an owner who is in a very strict routine, very consistent, and a strong character. These pups are quick to learn but also quick to test your training. I would never have one of these dogs, even if you paid me to!

Pup 3 - Friendly, middle of the pups, happy to be placed in any position, happy to be held in your arms belly up. Easy going, very accepting. Ideal dog for most if not all people. This pup will join in with anything that is going on but happily switch off otherwise. Ideal first dog, fairly intelligent, good to train (not as quick to learn as pup 1), will do ok at dog sports if trained well. If the owner is wanting to do dog sports or similar and doesn't have a strong confident character pup 3 is the one for them. This pup is affable, amenable and the best suited to a home with children. An ideal first dog. They are there to follow, to join in with the fun or the relaxation. This will be what I will be looking for when I look for my next puppy (I want an easier life this time!).

Pup 4 - Stays in the nest or runs back to it when visitors arrive, reserved, aloof, has its own agenda. Has a regal presence. Ideally should be with an owner who is a calm, confident person. If no other dog for it to live with it should spend the majority of its time with the owner/family. Without this it is likely to suffer severe separation anxiety. Highly intelligent, very quick to learn but will bore quickly with too much repetition. Trust in its owner is key. Not for the first-time dog owner as its quiet almost manipulative intelligence will outwit even the most experienced dog owner.

Pup 5 - Runs and hides behind mother, nervous, skittish and appears frightened. Ideal for someone who lives out in the countryside without many visitors or much going on in their life. This pup will bond very strongly to its owner but not have the confidence to bond with others. A great companion but doesn't do well in social settings. Low intelligence, its main drive in life is to bark to alert others of any changes in the environment and retreat to safety (usually behind its owner). This type of dog is often well suited to retired couples, who will spend most of their time with the dog opting for a slower pace of life.

The above is by no means a comprehensive list of common characters, and each individual will still develop personality and its experiences both with the litter and with you will help to shape it - but all will have a functional character too. Being aware of the different characters and how they will suit you, your knowledge level, lifestyle and personality can only help in your choice.

This may be controversial to some but if you look at people, we are much the same. Some are born to follow others, some to enforce the rules (policemen/women) and some are born leaders, managers, politicians etc. The qualities of which are usually seen when we are young and in school. Yes, some things we can learn to do but we will never be as practiced at them as someone who showed those traits in school and who have nurtured them over their lifetime.

If you want to know more about characters then I would suggest you buy another of my titles – Another Pup? As this goes into this subject in more detail (Link in chapter 20).

If you are unsure, video the pups playing, with you, with toys and with each other, drop your car keys or something similar near the litter (so it makes a strange noise) and watch how they react, who bounces back the quickest? Who avoids the keys or that area for a good while after? This way you can watch and analyse over and over at home.

If you are lucky enough to visit the litter when they are under three weeks of age, and still feeding from mum, take note of who is nearest the mother's back end, where do they feed on the milk bar?

The richest in nutrient teats are the furthest to the rear of the bitch, so you will often find pups 1, 2 & 4 with pups 3 & 5 at the teats closer to the bitch's chest. I must add though if the breeder interferes and places pups on teats, this will not show an accurate idea of character.

To pick the right puppy from the litter on character, it takes a few visits and some supporting information from the breeder, you need to build a picture of each pup and piece together the evidence.

Puppy Prepared?

16 PUPPY PLAN & GOALS

Have a plan, write down a description of what you want the ideal adult dog to be, how does it fit into your lifestyle, does it like curling up with you on the sofa, long hikes, playing ball? Do you plan to take it on holidays with you, either within the country or abroad, if abroad consider how you will travel, will it be on a ferry, a plane on the euro tunnel? All of these things need to be considered when making a plan for socialisation

Do you want your dog to come with you to visit family and friends? Are you likely to take your pup with you on long journeys? In a car? On a train?

Do you want to go to the pub or a café with your dog? Hotels, B&B's, tents, camper van, caravan? Do you want to compete with your dog in sports or showing?

When I got Ripple my goals and wishes for her went a little like this –

- Sociable with people, dogs and other animals.
- Happy go lucky accepting character, confidence.
- Of good 'type' for the breed as I wished to breed from

her subject to health tests etc.

- For her to have enough drive/energy to compete in dog sports and also be an ambassador for the breed, which is often mistaken as a barky, untrainable variety of dog.
- Loving and attentive.
- Must be good at travelling in vehicles, on my pony carriage, bonus would be if she liked to go on boats as Mark has always had them and we go through fits and spurts of having sea going trips.
- Adaptable to lots of different situations so we can go on holiday with her, I can take her to friends and families houses, B&Bs hotels etc. I think the best term here would be bombproof, I love to be involved in various activities at Crufts and that is a big thing for any dog to deal with, never-mind a little dog who simply sees a sea of feet and legs when in the crowds at Crufts.

From this I started to make a plan, it's all well and good having these goals, but without a plan to achieve them they were never going to happen.

Let's break a few of these down as an example –

Breeding – subject to all going to plan, it's not just a case of putting dog to bitch, waiting and then puppies arriving. Lots of handling of the bitch is involved, from taking temperatures to check how soon puppies will arrive (yes, shoving a thermometer up her backside) but also checking lady parts for the stage she is at in her season, with her breed it's advisable to hold her once the dog has tied to her during the mating process to avoid injury and considering her awkward long body shape. Essentially lots of physical handling and holding needed, above and beyond what you would need for the average pet dog who will not have puppies. So right from the start, the plan was to build a positive association with any kind of handling, so she expects good things when I touch her apart from the normal stroking. Starting gently with lots of treats and building from there, being mindful to keep doing this regularly as she grows and matures. Numerous trips to the vets just for practice so she would have a positive view on the vets – ensuring it wasn't scary.

Travelling – all of my dogs spend a considerable amount of time on the road with me, whether for work or for competitions, travelling fair distances. I currently have three vehicles, my van for work, with fitted cages, a little cheap 2-seater run-around and the pony lorry, all of which Ripple will be expected to travel in regularly. Added to this is riding on the carriage, without stress, noise or impatience. She was driven home in a car as will most puppies, ideally puppy should have already had a few car rides anyway with the breeder, to the vets etc but more work would be needed. With Ripple I knew she would be expected to settle while traveling not just in one way either, think about how you expect your dog to travel when it is adult, considering size etc. Ripple is obviously a very small breed but I knew I would expect her to travel in a soft crate, in a large fitted metal crate, a smaller one and also to relax on a harness fixed to a seatbelt both in the small car and in the lorry so lots of different ways for her to travel. It was/is likely at some point our vehicles will change and she will be expected to relax in the boot of a car too so all of this would need practice repetition and rewards.

Carriage driving – to allow her as much chance to get used to it as possible, starting young and on suitable roads (as large passing traffic may be scary to one so tiny initially) for shorter drives and often was the plan, which I did and it worked, she's the best out of all of them now to accompany us on carriage drives, no matter the weather or traffic we happen to be in. Even on very bumpy and bouncy terrain she is relaxed and often goes to sleep as she is so relaxed.

Sociable with people – all types of people, fat, thin, young, old, black white, with glasses and or beards and without, hats, loud, quiet etc. I lined up numerous short outings with her while she was still under 12 weeks, planned them and put them in my diary – to ensure I had this covered as this was a big priority. Of course, we still did lots after this point but under 12 weeks is the absolute priority as without this you are setting yourself and puppy up to fail. Outings such as carrying her in my arms to the pub, walking down the local high street (be prepared for everyone to stop you and comment on and want to touch puppy – more on this in the next book), attending a local dog show or event, attending a few different indoor dog training class environments, the local market etc.

Allow yourself some time off work - bonding with puppy

This is rather hypocritical of me as I was back at work a couple of days after Ripple came home - the difference here is that being self-employed means I have the flexibility I need for a puppy, and I work with dogs and dog people so I guess it's almost expected that everyone should get to see a new puppy. Ripple came everywhere with me and she was happy to do so as she was confident and happy to travel.

It is a stressful experience for a pup coming away from its mother, breeder and litter mates, you will need to be its security blanket and help it settle and feel confident in its new home.

You will also need to teach it how to be left alone and this takes a little time and patience. Going back to 9-5 without a plan for when leaving pup just a few days after they come, can be and often is a very stressful experience for the puppy and this can quickly turn into separation anxiety (especially if it is also at around 8 weeks of age and its going through its first fear period).

A week, ideally two off work to bond with puppy, to play, to carry it out and about to help socialise it and also to build up the time in which it is happy and settled when left. So please do not spend every waking minute with the puppy during this time either as that will not be helpful.

Consider whether you will need extra help for when you do need to leave the puppy for longer periods. Do you need a friend, family member or a professional to come in and see the puppy between times? Some planning will be needed for this too.

It's also worth popping round to the neighbours, explaining to them that a puppy will be arriving and ask for some patience while you get it settled in, apologise in advance if they can hear puppy through the walls. Reassure them that this will be only very short term and maybe even offer them a bottle of wine to sweeten the deal.

Plan for hard work

Plan for a year, minimum, of hard work! It will be closer to two for larger breeds and over two years for giant breeds. The cute sleepy puppy that is amazing in the first few weeks soon becomes a bundle of energy that will be taking up a lot of your time and energy. You will need to consider when you are taking holidays and whether you will be taking puppy with you, if not then where is it going to go while you are away and are, they going to do what you do with them?

A puppy's hormones start to kick in at 16 weeks of age, this means you have a teenager living with you who will test you and push boundaries until they reach maturity in adulthood. For a Labrador this could be 2.5-3 years of age. Smaller breeds mature quicker and larger breeds slower. Just because they are no longer classed as a puppy does not necessarily mean they are an adult either. When a bitch reaches its first season, or a male dog first cocks its leg this is merely sexual maturity... much like a 12-year-old girl or a 14-year-old boy. Neither of these adolescent humans would be expected to act like an adult at this age, so please do not expect your dog to.

I go into this in lots of detail, offering solutions to the problems you will face during this time in book 2 of the series. However, the problems and frustrations you will face will be a lot less than most if you follow each step in this book which will ensure you are getting your dream do, your super sidekick and your new best bud. Your new BFF that you will enjoy and cherish for many years to come!

Puppy Prepared?

17 PUPPY PROOFING YOUR HOME, WHERE THEY ARE ALLOWED TO GO & WHERE THEY ARE NOT

Management & prevention is so, so much better than the cure!

I want you to really sit down and think about this section, it can not only save your pups life it will also save you time, frustration and money if you get it right.

Puppies much like babies explore the world by putting things in their mouth! The difference is puppies come with tiny razor-sharp teeth that will cut through cables and such like in a matter of second which could potentially kill them in an instant! There are numerous parts to this.

Crate training

As I'm sure you have gathered by now, I am very pro crate training.

I get that this maybe a fairly alien subject to some.

Why would you want to put your dog behind bars? Is it not cruel?

What's the point in having a dog if you just shut it away? These are all things I hear from clients and dog owners regularly and I to ws one of those people once, so I get it!

Like any form of dog equipment if used wrong or abused, yes it can be a very cruel device, very cruel and damaging to a dog indeed.

If used in the right way it can half the time it takes to housetrain your puppy, both in terms of chewing things they shouldn't and with toilet training.

If used in the right way your pup will love going in their crate and see it as a safe place, a cave of sorts. Particularly if you have young children as well as a puppy it will be a great escape from the constant goings on of the household for a puppy that needs to switch off and sleep.

If your dog is ever unfortunate enough to have to have major surgery in future, having your dog crate trained can be an absolute blessing, even if you have not used a crate for years. This can manage the amount your dog is moving helping its period of recovery, both aiding its recovery and speeding up healing time.

You do not need to use a crate forever if you do decide to use one, most can be left loose without a crate before 12 months of age.

I get that crates don't exactly look nice, but they are invaluable in my mind to modern puppy training. If you want to splash out there are plenty of nicer style (without metal bars), confinement systems that you can purchase, in the style of nice wooden furniture etc. The metal wire type is the most commonly used and normally within most people's budget though again the larger the breed you choose the more this purchase will cost.

Although I have had many puppies of my own and trained them successfully both with and without a crate, I now opt for a crate and a puppy pen allowing pup to have more freedom while still not being able to get into trouble and chew or destroy things it shouldn't when you cannot be there or you cannot actively watch them.

A crate only needs to be big enough for pup to walk into, turn around and lay down. Having a suitable size crate will further speed up the toilet training process avoiding the temptation from the pup to toilet at one end and sleep at the other. However, depending on the size of the dog you choose you may opt to have a crate big enough for when it is fully grown and this is fine, it saves you buying multiple sizes, just be mindful of the unwanted temptation to toilet. If you can block off some of the space so pup cannot access all of it when it is very tiny. Many brands will sell a separate wire divider to allow you to do this. These dividers aren't often available in retail shops but are more widely available looking online.

Putting puppy in a crate should NEVER be done as a punishment. This should be a nice safe place for your pup to relax and sleep in. Feeding them in their crate can also speed up the process in which they accept and like the crate.

You can claim your free crate training guide by visiting my Facebook page (links at the end) or by emailing me.

Merlin's crate training paid off!

I used a crate with Merlin right from the day he came home and he accepted it fairly quickly, we used it until he was around 6 months of age when it was no longer needed (and I wanted more space in my tiny kitchen!), I could trust him to be left loose in the kitchen without fear of destruction. He often travelled in crates in my van but also travelled with a harness when in my car for a few years - but we did not use one in the house after that. When Merlin was just shy of 4 years of age, unfortunately he had to have a major spinal operation which meant strict crate rest for a few months while he recovered. He was a bouncy lad, very energetic anyway and was prone to doing too much. Especially with the addition of painkillers he thought he was on top form despite having 16 staples in his back at the time. We got the crate back out and he had to spend much of his time in there at least for the first month post operation. Only coming out to eat or toilet - on the vets advice. He accepted this straight away and was very relaxed in his little crate cave, bouncy when out and had to be supervised so he didn't hinder his recovery but having the history of him being crate trained paid off no end. We had another 6-7 years of joy with him and I know that this was a big part of that. If he had not been crate trained, he would have been very stressed at being expected to relax in a small space having never experienced something like that before.

Slippy floors

You are likely sick of me saying this by now, but this is a big issue that can so easily be avoided.

As I mentioned in the exercise section - having floors that are slippy are not good for a growing puppy, nor an adult dog.

Although great for cleaning up accidents and maybe cute to watch your pup slide around as they take a corner too fast etc it's not good for their skeletal developments nor their confidence. Consider whether you need to by some cheap non slip mats to help your pup get around. I say cheap due to risk of chewing and if pup has an accident on them. Ideally some that are small enough for you to put in the washer from time to time but also heavy enough that your pup does not get into the habit of pulling them around everywhere.

Areas of the house / Safety

Consider where you will want your dog to go and not go. No, your dog does not need to be able to go in every single room in the house, if you want that that's fine but I would suggest you consider housetraining, fouling on expensive rugs, carpets and chewing your beloved grandmothers dressing table. Even if you wish for your dog to have free roam when they are adult, they do not need to have free roam when they are a puppy and in fact restricting access to certain area will make your life a lot easier and in turn make it easier to train your puppy. My own dogs are not allowed free roam of the house, in fact 90% of the time they are restricted to our open plan kitchen, living room, diner and conservatory. These are the areas we spend the most time too so it's not as if they are shut out away from us all of the time. Carpets are upstairs, with hard flooring downstairs (handy for tiny bladders in case of any accidents), electric cables are either hidden or behind furniture without such a gap that a puppy could get behind them. You are not being mean by restricting your puppy to the kitchen or utility area, particularly if you are not around – this is damage limitation and setting you both up for success.

Things puppies love but we don't like them to love –

Electric cables
Wood – chair legs etc
Skirting board corners
Tv remotes
Rugs
Slippers/shoes
Our hands
Our feet
Fluffy dressing gowns and any item of clothing that flaps around
Sofa corners
Wicker baskets, chairs etc
Cushions
Paper/books/dvd cases
Anything that is left on the floor or within reach!!

In your puppy's eyes, everything is there to investigate and chew!
EVERYTHING!

So no matter how many toys and chews you buy for your pup they will still find something else to grab, chew, bite or wee on that you don't want them to, the more we restrict what they can get to that they shouldn't the better!

Short term, the tidier you can be with putting things away etc the better! You may need to think about temporarily boarding/blocking off little holes or gaps for behind the tv if you have one on a tv stand, pushing sofas back to walls if you have plugs behind, taking up rugs etc.

You can get 'anti chew' sprays to spray on things like soft furnishings and chair and table legs etc to discourage chewing. I have only found one such product that has the desired results for most if not all dogs. In 12 years of working with hundreds if not thousands of puppies and having my own for 14 years I have found that 'Grannicks bitter apple spray' is the most reliable but two puppies I have worked with have not been put off by it. Most if not all brands from mainstream pet shops I have found a less that 50% success rate so always recommend Grannicks. Its available on Amazon. Google will suggest various home remedies such as lemon juice, curry powder etc - again mixed results.

I would not simply rely on a spray to avoid damage. Sprays are more of an added extra with management being the number one thing. I didn't need to use Grannicks at all when raising Ripple as we had cracked the management and provided plenty of mental stimulation, chews, toys and training to keep her occupied and tired.

Using management/prevention is great and very important but we also need to provide puppy with things they are allowed to chew, I'm not just talking about toys either. Puppies NEED to chew, as to adult dogs, but puppies in particular. It's not just a want for them it's a need, and more so when they are teething which starts from 12 weeks and finishes at around 6 months. Chewing is a stress reliever and a pain reliever; it helps to tire them out mentally and provides great enrichment. The more we can provide tasty things for them to chew the less likely they are to apply their chewing instinct to things we would rather they didn't. Having a good supply of chews, stuffed Kongs and even home-made items for them to hew on is vital in this. Yes, they can chew on their toys also but providing something tasty makes them both less likely to want to chew items they shouldn't and helps to prevent the toy destruction too.

18 COMPETITIONS/ACTIVITIES

Most people buying their first dog will not have any vision or idea of competing with their dog. However, you may want to, so I have included a list of dog sports in the UK with a brief description of each. Dog sports are addictive and expensive, but very rewarding and a great way to bond with your dog. They are not for everyone and most sports are not in the public eye and you may not be aware of. Have a read through, one or two may appeal. Consider this with your choice of breed and your lifestyle.

I have competed in Breed showing, Rally and Obreedience. I have done all of these primarily with my dachshunds but have also done some with Merlin in the past. I have attended many training days for many sports to dip my toe as it were to see if it were something I might like to pressure and or my dogs may like to - for if they do not enjoy it then there is no point! So while I have a good idea on most sports I have asked others to give input into this chapter. They are credited at the end of each section or sport.

Massive thanks to all for your help on this!

Rally

A fairly new sport, the first KC rally competition was in April 2013 and I first competed later the same year with Moss.

My first judging appointment in Rally was the following year and I am now one of only a handful of KCAI Rally instructors for this fun and welcoming sport. My Dachs are the first of their breed to achieve the top level titles (Level 6).

A sport which welcomes all breeds and types and is suited well to all handlers also, including the disabled. A Rally course consists of various signs on a course which handlers and dogs navigate together, each sign with an exercise to perform. The lower levels being as simple as sit and the highest levels being more complex tasks such as control from a distance and formal retrieve of the handlers item which is placed on the floor by a scribe while the dog is not looking before the handler or owner sends them to retrieve said item.

The importance in Rally is put on loose lead walking and the connection between dog and handler. Progression through the levels is not through winning but from achieving 'qualifying scores'. What I personally like about this sport is that you are only competing against yourself, always trying to better your last score.

Level 1 is the entry level and achievable to most dog owners who are just starting out and have attended normal training classes with their dog. Rally is as much a challenge for the owner as the dog and keeps you thinking and on your toes.

It was originally a mixture of competitive obedience and agility. Whilst there are a few jump exercises still included they are under strict control and with a singular jump unlike agility. Many handlers in Rally do progress onto competing in competitive obedience and also in working trials, the skills needed for Rally are very much transferrable to other sports. Many handlers from other sports also then enter Rally competitions when their dog has retired from other sports.

Breed showing

There are two ways you can show your dog.

To participate in Open, Limited or Championship Kennel Club Shows, you need a Kennel Club Registered Pedigree dog. If you wish to show your dog, ensure you go to a breeder who also shows and is doing well with their own dogs in the show ring - this helps you know they are good examples of the breed. Secondly you will need to research a local 'Ring Craft' class which will teach you and your dog about how to stack (stand) correctly, how to encourage them to move nicely, and how to work together to show off the assetts of your dog. Avoid classes that use shake cans or spray bottles as these are not positive ways to train your puppy.

Shows have to be entered in advance, sometimes closing eight weeks prior to the show. On the day you will have to wait for your breed or group class. If you win your class, you will be invited back to 'Best of Sex' which is where everyone whose won a class in your breed (and gender) are judged against each other to determine 'the best'.

Best Bitch and Best Dog then compete against each other to crown 'Best of Breed'.

Best of Breeds usually then compete against other Best of Breeds at the end of the day for Best in Show!

The second option to showing your dog is open to any type of dog, pedigree, KC registered, crossbreed or mutt, and that is Companion or "fun" shows. Each type of show chooses their classes which can vary from "Best Pastoral" to "Best Sausage Catcher"! You can research these types of shows on your local dog groups on social media.

With thanks to Jeannie G - http://www.putyourpawsup.co.uk

Scent Work

Scentwork is a very new canine sport brought over from America. Tailored for all breeds and ages of pet dogs and their owners, it imitates the types of tasks carried out by professional handlers and their dogs in finding bombs, drugs etc. The dogs are trained to recognise specific scents and to search and find them. It is particularly accessible for "dogs who need space" as the dogs work individually in class and competition. It is a great way for dogs and handlers to bond as they work together. There are a number of organisations both national and more local which promote and organise the sport. Scentwork UK is one of the largest and most widely established. Go to their website to find out more and where the nearest trainer to you is located.

https://scentworkuk.com/
With thanks from Karen Kendal of RBC Petcare Banbury

Agility (the sport with the tunnel and jumps etc)

A dog sport that involves 1 dog and 1 handler to negotiate a series of obstacles on a course set by a judge to test speed and agility. Training and competing requires the dog and handler to have trained a selection of verbal commands and physical directions. Dog Agility is a perfect way to both dog and handler physically and mentally fit. It's a great way to meet new people and dogs with the same interests.

With thanks from Stuart Doughty -
https://stuartdoughtyagility.webs.com/

Bikejor

What is 'Bikejor'?

Bikejor is the sport of cross-country biking with your dog attached to your bike, it can be much faster and more exhilarating than canicross and is particularly suitable for dogs who really embrace running.

What do I need to start bikejoring?

Aside from the obvious (a mountain bike, safety equipment such as hat, glasses and gloves), you will need a comfortable fitting harness for your dog, an attachment for your bike and a long bungee lead to connect you both.

Dog Harness

The dog harness will take the pressure of pulling away from your dogs throat, which is essential if your dog is going to be pulling in front of your bike.

Bike Attachment

The attachment for the bike helps to prevent the line from dropping into the front wheel if your dog slows down or stops suddenly. It is not a fail-safe but will dramatically reduce the amount of tangles you have.

Bungee Line

The bungee lead is the shock absorbing element of your equipment and protects both you and your dog from the force of your dog pulling suddenly. When bikejoring, the line length needs to be longer than with canicross to help ensure your dog has enough space and is running clear of the front wheel.

A brief note on bikes

You can start bikejoring with any bike but one which is substantial enough for cross country riding is best. A basic 'hardtail' mountain bike is a great starting point. Brakes need to be good and many bikejorers prefer disc brakes as for safety reasons you will need to rely on them!

How do I start training for Bikejor?

The best way to start your training is by training voice commands on walks, decide early on what your left and right commands will be and try to get a good 'slow down' command from the outset. You can use your line or lead to guide your dog in the direction you want them to go and also physically slow them down when you use your 'steady' commands.

There are no hard and fast rules about what commands to use and people often use different ones, but traditional sled dog commands are based on:

Gee = Right turn

Haw = Left turn

Hike / Mush = Go forward (starts or encourages the dog to move)

On by = To pass another dog or team of dogs

Straight on = To stay straight on the trail if there are many options

Easy = Slow down

Whoa = Stop

Things you can do to encourage your dog to run out front:

Use a higher pitched voice to signal you would like them to up their energy and prepare them for activity. It might sound silly but dogs do respond to pitch changes in voice and if you raise this your dog will learn this means fun!

Go out in a group with more experienced dogs. Dogs learn from each other and will often naturally compete with their peers

Get someone to run or bike in front of you. Again, dogs naturally like to chase and by having someone in front of you, they may be more motivated to stay out front. You can even use a favourite toy to encourage your dog to fetch it.

However, try not to rely on this method and always encourage your dog to run independently because it is not always advisable to train your dog to chase! Use the method as a tool and work on building your dog's confidence.

You also need to check where you are allowed to train with a bike or scooter locally, as this can be more complex than canicross.

We recommend taking out some kind of sports insurance to cover yourself, when training and racing.

Some Forestry Commission land requires you to have a permit to train and these permits generally require £5 million public liability insurance.

The thing to remember is keep it short (at first), fun and safe, when you get more confidence you can then work on getting faster and even enter some races!

Canicross

The sport of Canicross is rapidly growing in the UK as more people discover it and the benefits it can bring for both human and canine alike.

Canicross in it's simplest form is running cross country (on trails and paths, rather than roads) with your dog and many people have been doing this with their dogs without even realising there is a name for it, or that it is a sport which has it's own competitions.

Why Canicross?

I've divided this into the 3 sections.

Behaviour - Many rescued and high energy dogs have benefitted from participating in outdoor pursuits with their owners such as running (Canicross) biking (Bikejor) and scootering in addition to the more established outdoor dog activities. The effect of activity is to allow your dog an outlet for energy which might otherwise be used for destructive and unwanted behaviours around the home & garden. Canicross is a great way to exercise a dog who can't otherwise be let off lead due to (among other things) a high hunting instinct, which is why you will see many different breeds participating from terriers to malamutes.

Health - Recent studies estimate that as many as one third of dogs nationwide are overweight and this figure is set to rise to over half of all dogs by 2022. Obesity is linked with diabetes, orthopaedic disease, heart disease, respiratory distress, high blood pressure, skin diseases & cancer (much the same as in people) so you might even be prolonging your own life as well as your dog's with consistent exercise!

Fun - Taking part in dog sports usually means you and your dog get to socialise with likeminded people but even if it's just you and your dog, you will be strengthening your bond with your dog which is very rewarding and great fun too.

What do I need to Canicross?

The basic kit for canicrossing properly is a comfortable, well-fitting harness for your dog, a bungee line to absorb the shock from any pull for both you and your dog and a waist belt so you are hands free when running. These 3 main elements form the basis for a pleasant experience when running with your dog. Without the harness you risk pulling on your dog's neck, without the bungee you can find yourself jerked after something interesting on your route and without the waist belt you may find your neck, shoulders and back ache from holding a lead.

What harness?

There is now a huge variety of choice for all sizes and shapes of dogs, with new products being brought out regularly. Which harness is best suited for your dog depends on a number of factors but at K9 Trail Time we offer a free consultation to help get you started in the right direction.

What line?

As long as there is bungee for shock absorption then most lines will be fine. Some are made from webbing and some from stronger polypro braid but which you choose is personal preference. The standard canicross lines are approximately 2 metres when stretched but many people run with shorter or longer lines based on their own requirements. Some races have rules on line length, so do ask if you're thinking of competing in Canicross

What waist belt?

The style of waist belt which you choose is down to what you would like from it and what you find most comfortable. The basic things you need to ask yourself are: Do I want something padded or lightweight? Do I want leg straps? Do I want pockets? Once you know the answer to these then it makes choosing a belt much easier. The purpose of the belt is for your comfort and to ensure canicrossing with your dog does not damage your back, shoulders, neck or arms.

How do I get started?

The best way to get started is to find a group of people locally who are already canicrossing, as there are many social groups now encouraging new people to join them. A group will most likely have spare kit they could loan you to kit to try out and will be able to offer advice about training your dog with voice commands for directions etc.

Lastly, but most importantly, your dog needs to be fit and fully developed before you begin canicrossing. Most races will not allow a dog under 1 year old to compete and it is recommended you start your dog off very gently at around the year-old stage and not before. You also have to ensure you will be putting your dog's health first and to avoid any problems, stick to running in cool temperatures (never in the heat of the day in summer) and carrying water with you in case your dog needs it.

If you would like any more information on Canicross or the equipment you need to begin please do contact Emily at K9 Trail Time and she will be happy to help you. There is also a lot of information on her website www.k9trailtime.com and on her wordpress blog.

Canicross and Bikejor information are both provided by and with many thanks to Emily Thomas

Hoopers

Hoopers is a low impact, low cost, fun activity that any dog can try. The dogs will pass through a series of hoops, around or past barrels and through tunnels. The hoop and barrel size are standard across most countries, the tunnels used in European style hoopers are 80cm diameter and 100-300cm long, rather than agility tunnels that are 60cm diameter and 300-500cm long.

Classes are mainly split into the following categories', Hoopers which is purely hoops. Barrelers which is predominantly barrels, tunnelers which is mainly tunnels and Mixed which is hoops, barrels and tunnels. There is no jumping involved in any of the categories, which is what adds to the appeal. Hoopers helps with the dog's proprioception. Builds teamwork and trust between dog handler, provides both mental and physical exercise and most importantly is fun for dogs and their handlers.

Hoopers is one of these most inclusive sports you can try with your dog. Hoopers can be tried by any age handler and dog team, you can handle from a distance or move more with your dog which ever style works for the team Hoopers is open to all. From Dachshunds to Danes any breed can try Hoopers. Younger dogs can start to build confidence and improve their listening skills, it's a great way to teach direction and to give your dog a job. Hoopers provides mental and physical stimulation so is also appealing to those with older dogs that may not be able to compete at other dog sports due to the intensity. Elements of Hoopers can be easily practiced at home or at the local park.

For more information on Hoopers please visit www.caninehoopersworld.com or visit the Facebook page @caninehoopersworld

With thanks from Carrie-Anne Selwyn

Dog Parkour

A great way to build a bond with your puppy and help them grow in confidence with while getting out and exploring the environment. Dog Parkour is a non-competitive sport where you and your dog work as a team for your dog to safely interact with obstacles you find on your everyday walk. Your puppy can step onto a kerb, balance along a low wall, duck under a tree branch - the possibilities are endless. The IDPKA (International Dog Parkour Association) offer titles which guide your Parkour journey. You can work towards the initial, low impact "Training Title" as soon as your puppy comes home and the foundation skills you learn will carry you through your dog's lifetime.

Contact details: dogparkour.org is the website of the founding organisation the International Dog Parkour Association

With thanks From Rachel Bradley

Obedience

You and your dog working together as one in a seamless partnership with exercises to show precision and accuracy.

It is the training that really gives you and your dog the fun and enjoyment of working together. It builds a close bond, great rapport, a high level of communication with each other and you learn a lot about your dog and yourself.

The competing gives you a goal or purpose to the training and it is just you and your dog doing your best in a supportive, inclusive and competitive sport.

Obreedience

Working with a team of like-minded people all with the same passion for their breed to proudly show what that breed can achieve.

You are not alone, and team spirit is key. Training together and sharing knowledge to bring the best out of each individual dog and supporting each other. The dogs get to interact with the team, both human and canine, and importantly have fun and friendships are forged.

Competing gives you chance to proudly show what your breed can achieve as part of a team, you have support and camaraderie in a friendly sport.

Both sports above are with thanks from Jo Stanley - one of my lovely Dachtastic Obreedience team members

Flyball

In short, Flyball is a high speed relay race between two teams of dogs.

The name of the game is for each dog to pass the start line, run down a set of four jumps to the "box", trigger the box to collect their ball and then run over the four jumps back to their handler while holding the ball over the start line. The next dog must not cross the start line until the other dog has reached the start line. This is called the "cross over". The winning team is the one whose four dogs complete their runs cleanly without errors in the fastest time.

In competition, each team will usually face four to six other teams in competition throughout a day, that are of similar "seed time". A teams seed time is determined by their fastest time from previous shows, or can be "declared" but that's where it starts to get complicated.

The "box" is very important. It holds the tennis balls. The most efficient way of triggering the box and collecting the ball is called a "swimmers turn". This is where the dog is able to rebound/ jump onto the box using all four feet AND catch the ball. It is a very technical and elegant move.

A team is made up of four to six dogs, with only four required to run in each race, but can be swapped in and out between the six declared on the team sheet. The shortest dog of the four running is known as the "height dog" as the jumps are set to that dog's level. A speedy height dog can be a team's most valuable asset!

In the UK, we have two main organisations that run flyball. The long established BFA, and the newer UKFL. Both have the same fundamental game but with slightly different rules making each organisation more unique, such as width of the jumps and how they determine the heights a dog will run.

If you wish to try flyball, it is highly advised you find an established and experienced team, as taught incorrectly, or too young, can have a negative impact on a dog's joints. Flyball is a very inclusive team sport but be prepared for the noise!

With thanks to Jeannie G - http://www.putyourpawsup.co.uk

Heelwork To Music

A fairly new sport which mixes elements of Obedience and Agility with your favourite music! Choose your track, no minimum length in time, but Starters maximum music is just 2minutes and 30 seconds, start playing the music over and over whilst training and put together a routine using your dog's favourite moves!

HTM is split into two divisions:

Heelwork To Music – where the dog does an Obedience style heelwork but can work on you left and right facing forwards or backwards and across your front and back in both directions! The music must be choreographed to show pauses, rhythm and different paces.

Freestyle – spins, weaves, jumps are the good base moves needed for freestyle. Match your dog's moves to the music and make your way around the ring having good fun! If you can keep your dog with you for at least 2 minutes, moving with your music and incorporating moves your dog loves to do, then you are well on your way to HTM success!

With thanks from Kath Harman for the information.

Man trailing

Trailing is really amazing; it is unbelievable how quickly all breeds pick this up. You start with short trails to find a person. The dog is offered the scent of the person to find. With that person visual, massive rewards from the found person. Moving on to longer trails person hidden.

It is great to watch your dogs do what comes naturally to them, using their noses. You are on the end of a long line with them on a harness, you fully have to trust your dog as you have no idea where the person is. You learn how to read your dog better. You will understand how they work, either ground or air scenting or both. Usually they will use both methods. If you wish you can then move on to register as a handler with a dog that can help find missing people or dogs or just continue to work, your best friend doing what comes naturally to them.

With thanks from Sue Wood

Working Trials

A competitive sport based on the civilian equivalent of police dog work. They develop and test many canine skills - obedience and control, intelligence and independence, searching and tracking, agility and fitness. Trials are physically demanding for both dog and handler but are also great fun and extremely rewarding.

Working Trials tests are broken down into three main sections:

1. Nosework

Nosework comprises search and track exercises. The dog follows a track laid by a 'tracklayer' (who is a stranger to the dog) walking a set pattern designed by the judge and identical for each dog. The track is approximately half a mile long and laid on grassland, arable fields or heathland with each competitor working on similar terrain to others in the stake. As the dog follows the track it has to seek out and recover articles placed along the track by the tracklayer. The track is laid at different times, before the dog work begins, depending on the level of the competition. The other component of nosework is 'search' where the dog has to search for and retrieve articles placed in a marked area.

2. Agility

To test its agility, the dog must clear three obstacles - a three-foot hurdle, a six foot high wooden scale and a nine foot long jump. Two attempts may be permitted for each obstacle.

3. Control

There are various exercises in this section which are detailed below:

Heelwork - the dog must walk with its shoulder reasonably close to the handler while the handler navigates their way around people and obstacles at different speeds.

Sendaway - involves sending the dog away across a minimum distance of 50 yards, the handler will then redirect the dog through a series of commands.

Retrieving a Dumbbell - the dog must retrieve a dumbbell which has been thrown by the handler.

Down Stay - the dog must stay in the down position while the handler is out of sight for a period of time.

Steadiness to Gunshot - the dog is tested on its reactions to gunshot. The dog will be penalised if it shows any signs of fear or aggression.

Speak - the dog is ordered to "speak" and cease "speaking" on command by the handler with a minimum of commands and/or signals.

With thanks from the Kennel Club - https://www.thekennelclub.org.uk/activities/working-trials/new-to-working-trials/

IPO/Schutzhund

IPO, formerly known as Schutzhund (literally translated as "protection dog"), was originally developed as a breed suitability test for the German Shepherd Dog. In the early days, German Shepherds were considered the ultimate working dog. While it eventually turned into a German dog sport, it has since evolved further into the largest protection sport competition in the world. Considered the triathlon for dogs, IPO is a three phase sport that tests a dog's temperament and physical soundness for work and breeding.

While initially only German Shepherd Dogs were eligible, any breed can now compete in the sport. However, it's very rare to see a breed that has not been bred specifically for work to do well. Most commonly, you'll find German Shepherds, Belgian Malinois, Rottweilers, Dutch Shepherds and Dobermans competing successfully. These dogs have many generations of bloodlines created to maintain the temperament necessary for serious work. While IPO is a sport, the dogs it tests and promotes are used for police and military work. It is nearly impossible to find rescue dogs that can successfully compete and fight a perpetrator the way these dogs can.

The protection phase is the most iconic phase in IPO. It consists of the dog and handler team and a perpetrator called a helper. The helper wears a protective sleeve over his arm to keep him safe when the dog attacks. In IPO, dogs are specifically taught to attack the forearm of the helper. There are various exercises in the protection phase, such as a blind search for the helper and a full-field attack. Each exercise shows different aspects of the dog's mental stability and willingness to fight.

Protection is not the only phase in IPO. Equally important are the other two: tracking and obedience. Tracking is done with the dog following the scent of his handler or a stranger. The dog works at a 10 meter distance from the handler, and the handler must follow the dog as he guides him along the track. Depending on the level the team is competing in, the tracks are 100-600 paces and contain a number of articles the dog must locate. Articles are any piece of leather or other material that are hidden on the track. The dog must not only find them, but indicate them to the handler by lying down. Tracking demonstrates the search and rescue capabilities of the dog, as well as his concentration and focus on daunting tasks for extended periods. *With thanks from* https://iheartdogs.com/dog-sports-101-iposchutzhund/

Disc Dog

Disc dog, which is also called frisbee dog, is a type of dog sport which uses discs. Most of the disc dog competitions are distance catching and choreographed freestyle catching. A team of one dog and one person can compete in the "toss and fetch" event. Points are awarded for certain distances.

Some of these competitions involve the dynamic freestyle event, which consists of choreographed techniques with music and with multiple discs on display. There are categories based on skills and experiences of the handler, but the long distance category is divided by gender.Some other popular events are toss and fetch, freestyle, and long distance. The toss and fetch is a mini-distance throw and catch event. The contestant can make as many throws within 60 seconds. The freestyle competition is a judged event, with routines lasting up to 1 minute and 30 seconds. The long distance event used to be just a half time show in the NFL.

With thanks from https://www.topendsports.com/sport/list/disc-dog.htm

Pets As Therapy / PAT Dogs

This is not a sport but it is an activity that you may want to do with your dog and it's a very worthwhile and rewarding way to volunteer with your dog.

Thousands of people of all ages benefit every week from the visits provided by our Volunteer PAT Teams, dogs (who have been assessed) and their owners who visit residential homes, hospitals, hospices, schools, day care centres and prisons. Volunteers with just a small amount of spare time each week work with their own pets, to bring joy, comfort and companionship to many individuals who appreciate being able to touch and stroke a friendly animal.

All breeds of dogs can become part of a PAT Team, they must have been with their owner for at least 6 months, be over 9 months of age and be able to pass the temperament assessment. Regular visits are generally appreciated, although our volunteers agree upon how much time they generously give directly with the establishment they visit. There is no minimum or maximum time commitment although our pets should not work for more than 2 hours at any one time and need regular breaks.

With thanks from https://petsastherapy.org/what-we-do/

Working Your Gundog on a Shoot & Competitive Field Trials

On a typical shoot day there are three groups of people who all work together to ensure a successful day.

- The beaters job is to drive the birds towards the guns. They often have dogs to help them and most often these will be spaniels (springer or cocker) although other breeds are often seen.

- The pickers up wait behind the gun line until shooting is finished then they send their dogs to find and retrieve shot birds. It is particularly important that any injured birds are found quickly so they can be humanely despatched. The pickers up use Retrievers (Labrador, Golden, Flatcoat) but again other breeds can be used on smaller shoots. Most pickers up work a team of two or more dogs to get the job done quickly and efficiently.

- The guns are there to shoot but often they will bring a dog with them. Known as a peg dog, this animal is expected to sit quietly while shooting is taking place then, when the drive is over, is released to find birds shot by its owner.

It is important that any dog taken into the shooting field is quiet, steady on and off lead and responsive to verbal and whistle commands. In other words, the dog must be trained to a high standard for the job it will be asked to do.

While shooting only takes place in the autumn and winter, training takes place all year round and in the summer months many people like to take part in Gundog working tests to assess how their training is going. The highest level of competition for Gundogs is a Field Trial, which takes place on a shoot using live game.

With thanks from Heather Harley

19 **CONCLUSION**

Yes, there really is that much that goes into getting the dream dog!

When I started to write this book, books one and two were to be just one title. However the more I thought about it, the more there was to tell you about both getting the right puppy in the first place and also to getting the first year with puppy right, so I opted to split it into two. I expected this book to be half the size it is! It was not my intention to write a 50k word count of a book. But I dearly hope you have found it helpful - these are all things I am always advising people to do and now, finally it can help more puppies and owners and possibly breeders too.

Remember no dog is perfect, it's about getting the perfect puppy for you. The work doesn't stop here either, it has barely started! Having a puppy is a wonderful time full of smiles and cuteness, but it is just as much hard work - if not more. It's tiring, it's frustrating at times but if you follow the right advice and put the work in you will get there and it will all be worth it!

I can promise you that you will have moments of 'what the hell did we do?' 'why did we get a puppy?' 'please just do what I ask this one time, I'm tired!' but they will be brief if you have followed all the steps and considered all the points in this book and the next which is covering everything you need to know in your first year with pup.

By following my advice, you will be avoiding more dogs ending up in rescue and you will be supporting the great breeders. The breeders who put their heart and soul into their pups, so you have a happy confident dog for its lifetime.

I dearly hope you have learnt from my many mistakes.

Would I change any of it? No.

It has made me the person, the dog owner and the dog trainer I am today which helps me to help others, like you.

Will I make these mistakes again? Hell no!

In fact, I have my name down on a litter due to be born in the summer of 2020. A new Flatcoat puppy, exciting and very tiring times ahead. I'm well practiced with having Dach pups, but not so much with flatty pups. As much as Merlin was my heart dog, the first two to three years with him were extremely hard work! It's a wonder I had any hair left while he was young.

I allow 8-10 months of intensive work with a Dach from the time they come home, that I can plan for fairly easily. However big breed puppies take longer to mature, plus this particular breed is known for not maturing mentally, ever…a minimum of two years of intense work ahead. I was not a dog trainer when I first got Merlin, but I became one while he was young. I have built up lots of experience and knowledge over the last 10 years, but I am still a little nervous of a new one. Nervous of what new challenges they will bring and what lessons they will teach me. Nervous but excited. I dearly miss my boy, and despite me being known as 'the crazy Daxy lady', the fact remains that I'm a big dog person at heart. My home and life feels very empty without a big black duffus of a dog to keep me smiling.

You may want to consider helping out with something called Generation Pup. This is something that you can report on your puppy at each stage of its development for research purposes. You would be helping dogs and owners of the future and you can find out more here - https://generationpup.ac.uk/

Here is as a final recap, a quick run-down, your road map to getting your dream dog!

Research

- Breed groups

- Breeds

- Purposes of your chosen breed & instincts

- Temperaments

- Health problems

- Breeders

- Litters

- Local dog training classes

Consider

- Timing of puppy arriving

- If that breed is in fact the right fit for you

- Financial costs/budgets

- Time investment

- Waiting

- The mother's temperament

- The size of your vehicle

- Which puppy within the litter is right for you?

- If you need to provide your dog with a 'job' or outlet for its instincts

- How much grooming is required?

- Consider how long you expect to have the dog in your life…what is their expected lifespan? (remember this in those moments that you get impatient)

Don't rush, be picky, enjoy and good luck!

20 **LINKS & RESOURCES**

Get your free tips sheets for when puppy comes home and bonuses here!
https://mailchi.mp/houndhelpers/puppyprepared

Stay up to date with new books, releases and news -
https://www.facebook.com/SarahBartlettDogTrainer/

Another Pup? By the same author -
https://www.amazon.co.uk/dp/1720027161/ref=cm_sw_em_r_mt_dp_U_fzWYDbRJ22MXD

KC resource for helping you find the right breed for you -
https://www.thekennelclub.org.uk/services/public/findabreed/Default.aspx

Raw feeding veterinary society for more advice and information on raw feeding - https://rfvs.info/

Discover Dogs event in London (October) -
https://www.discoverdogs.org.uk/

Crufts (March) at the NEC Birmingham -
https://www.crufts.org.uk/

Puppy Culture find a breeder -
https://shoppuppyculture.com/pages/worldwide-breeder-map-on-vacation

Puppy Culture Exercise guidelines -
https://www.puppyculture.com/new-exercise-chart.html

Coi % -Mykc.org

Find a dog KC registered training club -
https://www.thekennelclub.org.uk/services/public/findaclub/

Dogs trust membership for public liability -
https://www.dogstrust.org.uk/get-involved/membership/

Guidelines for professional dog walkers -
https://www.dogstrust.org.uk/news-events/news/dog%20walking%20guide%20online.pdf

Find a dog sport - https://www.thekennelclub.org.uk/activities/

ENS - https://breedingbetterdogs.com/article/early-neurological-stimulation

Champdogs - https://www.champdogs.co.uk/

Find KC registered puppy -
https://www.thekennelclub.org.uk/services/public/findapuppy/

WSAVA guidelines -
https://www.wsava.org/WSAVA/media/Documents/Guidelines/WSAVA-Vaccination-Guidelines-2015.pdf

VacciCheck (vet, in house, cost effective blood test for immunity to three core diseases) - http://www.vaccicheck.com/

Adverse reactions to vaccinations reporting -
https://www.vmd.defra.gov.uk/AdverseReactionReporting/Product.aspx?SARType=Animal&AspxAutoDetectCookieSupport=1

Worm testing - https://wormcount.com/

PDSA Cost statistics - https://www.pdsa.org.uk/taking-care-of-your-pet/looking-after-your-pet/puppies-dogs/the-cost-of-owning-a-dog

Dog food quality checker - https://www.allaboutdogfood.co.uk/

Catherine O'Driscoll; What vets don't tell you about vaccines book https://www.amazon.co.uk/dp/B00S8S7ZC2/ref=cm_sw_em_r_mt_dp_U_SM-YDb81Y6FR6

.

Puppy Prepared?

ABOUT SARAH BARTLETT

A qualified dog training instructor specialising in multi-dog households, reactive/barky dogs, and puppy training. A Kennel Club Accredited Instructor in companion dog training and KC Rally. QIDTI – qualified international dog training instructor. Sarah has been professionally training dogs for eight years. Her company Hound Helpers Ltd was launched in 2007, which has helped thousands of dogs over that time.

She is based between Evesham and Pershore in Worcestershire but is proud of her Yorkshire roots. She enjoys spending her free time competing in KC Rally and Obreedience with her Dachshunds, doing various horse sports and activities including competitive carriage driving with her Fell Pony, Billy.

Sarah writes monthly articles for her local paper the Evesham Journal. She is also a monthly content contributor for the international magazine Edition Dog, and also the enrichment subscription box - The Canine Brain Box.

More book titles are always in the pipeline as she loves to help more people and dogs.

Keep up to date with what she's up to by searching @sarahbartlettdogtrainer on Facebook

She is often delivering workshops and talks around the UK too, you will find details of these on the Facebook page.

Author of -
Another Pup? The Comprehensive Guide to adding to or Becoming a Multidog Household

Printed in Great Britain
by Amazon